Who's in Charge Here?

We like to think that we are sensible beings who base our actions on conscious decisions. The fact is, all of us are subject to the occasional irrational impulse, the "wild hair" that surprises us and those around us. Usually, this is not a big problem—in fact, it can act as a safety valve for our creative abilities and a check against unnecessary self-restriction.

But it's not so healthy when we find ourselves driven by compulsions and obsessions that seem to take over our lives and consume our attention and energy. How can we discover the origins of these forces? Can we turn them into something constructive?

Astrology provides a key to these questions in the quindecile. This newly researched 165° aspect of hidden driving forces is thoroughly explored in these pages by an experienced astrologer and mental health professional. Numerous chart examples support the analysis of the quindecile in natal, transit, progressed, and synastry horoscopes. A full set of delineations and interpretations lets you quickly add this illuminating factor to your understanding of any chart.

About the Author

Ricki Reeves (Michigan) teaches astrology and lectures throughout North America. She has worked in the field of mental health, addictions, and recovery for more than ten years. She is a graduate of Noel Tyl's master's level astrology course.

To Write to the Author

If you wish to contact the author or would like more information about this book, please write to the author in care of Llewellyn Worldwide and we will forward your request. Both the author and publisher appreciate hearing from you and learning of your enjoyment of this book and how it has helped you. Llewellyn Worldwide cannot guarantee that every letter written to the author can be answered, but all will be forwarded. Please write to:

Ricki Reeves
⅞ Llewellyn Worldwide
P.O. Box 64383, Dept. 1-56718-562-2
St. Paul, MN 55164-0383, U.S.A.

Please enclose a self-addressed stamped envelope for reply,
or $1.00 to cover costs. If outside U.S.A., enclose
international postal reply coupon.

Many of Llewellyn's authors have websites with additional information and resources. For more information, please visit our website at http://www.llewellyn.com

The Astrology & Psychology of Obsession

THE
QUINDECILE

Ricki Reeves

2001
Llewellyn Publications
St. Paul, Minnesota 55164-0383, U.S.A.

First Edition
First Printing, 2001

Background cover photo © Digital Stock
Book design by Donna Burch
Cover design by Anne Marie Garrison
Editing by Andrea Neff

Library of Congress Cataloging-in-Publication Data
Reeves, Ricki, 1947–
    The quindecile : the astrology & psychology of obsession / Ricki Reeves.—1st ed.
      p. cm.
    Includes bibliographical references and index.
    ISBN 1-56718-562-2
     1. Quindecile (Astrology) 2. Obsessive-compulsive disorder—Miscellanea. I. Title.

BF1717.22.Q55 R44 2001
133.5—dc21   00-067232

Llewellyn Publications
A Division of Llewellyn Worldwide, Ltd.
P.O. Box 64383, Dept. 1-56718-562-2
St. Paul, MN 55164-0383, U.S.A.
www.llewellyn.com

Printed in the United States of America

Contents

Part I
The Psychology of Obsession

Chapter 1
The Psychological Dynamics
of Obsessive-Compulsive Behavior

Chapter 2
Obsession and Compulsion
as Opportunity versus Difficulty

Part II
An Astrological Overview of the Quindecile

PART III
Astrological Analysis of the Quindecile

Chapter 6
Dynamics of Natal Interpretation

Chapter 7
Activation Through Progression and Transit

Chapter 8
Synastry

PART IV
Index of Quindecile Delineations

Horoscopes

Foreword

Discoveries are exciting: something new is in our vision, in our way of doing things. We feel insight, we feel advancement, we feel uplifted. We feel improved that this has happened to us! That's what the *quindecile* is (quin-deh-chee'-leh): it's a "refound" aspect in astrology.

As the initial facilitator of this discovery, I have given the aspect the name of quindecile (15 in Latin—the 24th harmonic, the family of 15° increments), *pronounced the Italian way*. My strong recommendation for this pronunciation is an effort to capture the passion, the insistence, and indeed the obsession connoted by this aspect in our horoscopes and in our lives. Anything less than this approach, I think, would diminish this aspect, sterilize it, and ignore its representative power.

Chances are high that eight out of ten of you reading these words have one or two quin-deh-chee'-leh aspects in your horoscope. What is surprising is that, for so long in astrology, this dynamic aspect has gone relatively unnoticed. Now, with it known and activated, as it were, throughout much of the world, it is like learning a new vocabulary word: we begin to see and hear it everywhere. The discovery is also a surprise—it's been there all along!

After initially testing some 400 examples of the aspect (now over 1,000) in real-life situations, I passed on the concept to students in my Master's Degree Certification Course. Over 200 astrologers then took the quindecile further through their interaction with clients.

Soon, a large mass of evidence for this 165° aspect was accumulated. The quindecile entered mainstream astrology.

"How did we ever do without it?"—I have heard this so many times, in the excitement of discovery. For example, without the four quindecile aspects in Arnold Schwarzenegger's horoscope (July 30, 1947 at 4:10 A.M. CED in Graz, Austria) or the four quindecile aspects in General Norman Schwarzkopf's horoscope (August 22, 1934 at 4:45 A.M. EST in Trenton, NJ), how can we possibly understand the extraordinary drive to fame these men have achieved? In Marilyn Monroe's horoscope (June 1, 1926 at 9:30 A.M. PST in Los Angeles, CA), the quindecile between her Saturn retrograde and her Mercury in Gemini is an essential harbinger of her deep strain of depression and upset.

What about the Sun-Pluto quindecile in our national horoscope (July 4, 1776)? What about the subgeneration of men born with the Saturn-Pluto quindecile showing an increased and earlier occurrence of prostate cancer!

Discoveries are exciting indeed: they do help us do our job better. We are able to understand more, develop more, project more energies into the future, all on behalf of our clients. In turn, the people we serve with astrology learn more about the developmental tensions and need orientations of their lives. Discoveries help everyone; we all grow.

In my teaching program throughout sixteen countries, I see many, many astrologers growing at different rates of learning, into different areas of expertise. In the beginning, of course, *everything* in astrology seems to be an exciting discovery, and then, with skill and seasoning, the excitement is reserved for something new, something especially sophisticated.

One of my graduated students is Ricki Reeves, the author of this first-of-its-kind book. This is no surprise. Besides watching Ricki become a first-class astrologer, who now can stand with any in our world, I watched as well as she developed a *specialty*. That specialty is based upon a highly cultivated, natural empathy with others, an uncanny identification with the life situations that grip people strongly, that fight them or fortify them. Ricki is an expert at understanding addiction and obsession, at helping others break the routine in life before the life itself is broken by it. Time and time again, I watched as Ricki, in a simple, uncluttered way, opened up new pathways for her clients. The quindecile fit front and center into Ricki's technique. How could she ever have done without it?

It was the greatest pleasure to urge her on to further research about the quindecile, to discuss her findings with her, and to urge her to write this book.

Remembering that this book is now a big part of the quindecile discovery, we can see it also as a beginning: how will astrologers add to it in their experience? How will we refine all this information further?

You are now part of a research movement! And this book by Ricki Reeves is your guide. What a discovery—Ricki and this book!

—Noel Tyl

Acknowledgments

The writing of this book has been a journey of awareness for me. It has brought me face to face with my own obsessive-compulsive tendencies more than once. Without the support of family and friends, I truly don't know if I would have survived the experience.

My gratitude goes out to my Chicago family, who lived through this process day in and day out without complaint or criticism; Peggy Martin, who read and reread this material with an editor's eye; Donna Callaghan, who worked closely with me on the psychology of obsession and compulsion; and Carol White, who assisted me with the research.

A special thank you goes out to my astrological mentors who have encouraged me since this process began: Carole Ray, who mentored me as a young, inexperienced student of astrology and gave of her time and expertise to educate me in what has become my life's passion; and Noel Tyl, who first introduced me to the concept of the quindecile, and without whose extraordinary confidence, continual support, and encouragement I would not have believed that I could actually write this book.

Last, but certainly not least, my gratitude and love go out to my husband, David Hasenauer, who has given me the kind of unconditional love and support that I have never experienced before. He made sure that I ate, slept, and had whatever I needed to get through this process. To him I dedicate this book.

Introduction

Have you ever asked yourself "Why do I feel driven to be in a relationship? . . . to prove myself over and over again at work? . . . to make my children the center of my universe? . . . to eat or drink more than I know is good for me?" . . . and so on. Do you have a feeling that if you just try a little harder, then whatever it is you are trying to do will finally work out, believing that you are indispensable in making it happen? Does focusing so much of your time and attention on one particular area of life keep you from being able to enjoy a well-balanced, healthy lifestyle? If your answer to any of these questions is "yes," then you may be one of the millions of us who have some degree of obsessive-compulsive tendency.

Obsessive-compulsive behavior is defined as "recurrent obsessions or compulsions sufficiently severe to cause marked distress, be time-consuming, or significantly interfere with the person's normal routine, occupational functioning, or usual social activities or relationships with others."[1]

Well, I don't know about you, but my life frequently gets off track because of things that "cause me distress, become time consuming, and significantly interfere with my normal routine, occupational functioning, or usual social activities or relationships with others." So, does this mean that I have some deep psychological problem creating these situations, or is this simply the way my life goes?

The concept of being labeled "obsessive-compulsive," or even thinking of ourselves in this light, can be pretty daunting. The term "obsessive-compulsive" induces visions of extreme psychiatric diagnosis, marking one as dysfunctionally different from the "normal" person. We've been taught that these particular characteristics are not only antisocial, but should be locked away or medicated to the point of oblivion. Our society does love to maximize everything, doesn't it? If a particular tendency or behavior is the least little bit off the bell curve then it had better be changed, fixed, regulated, or better yet, cured. Isn't it those parts of our character that are somehow just a little different from everyone else that make us the special, unique human beings that we are? Do they not provide us with our own distinctive personalities? I, for one, say, "Let us celebrate our differences and channel those differences to create our own facets of individuality in the most beneficial manner possible!"

This is not to diminish or minimize the pain, suffering, and difficulty that people who have the true clinical diagnosis of obsessive-compulsive disorder must live with each and every day of their lives. It is, however, within that awareness that we must recognize that there are degrees of extremity into which this behavior can manifest. Most of us have some degree of obsessive-compulsive inclination wired into our instinctual databank. These tendencies are then demonstrated throughout our lives in various forms of behavior, action, or attitude. The effects of this can result in a wide range of possibilities: from a consummate drive to reach certain goals for an eventual positive outcome, to a complete fixation that blocks out everything else and propels us into a life that is completely devoted to that which is unattainable. The overall effects, experienced by each individual, are determined by the degree and manner in which the obsession and compulsion manifest, combined with the magnitude of disruption and separation created in the balance of our lives.

In these days of psychological awareness, we search endlessly for answers to why we do what we do, trying to find the hidden motivation that propels us in the directions that our lives take. We look to psychologists, therapists, or counselors; we read self-help books and join organizations that work with understanding behavior and the modification of behavior. Some of us even work with astrology and astrologers, and have been amazed when they seem to know everything about us without ever having met us before.

In astrology, we know that the horoscope references all the life dynamics, possibilities, and probabilities of the individual, and this particular psychodynamic, involving obsessive-compulsive tendency, is no exception. My study explores the identification, delineation, and understanding of these inclinations and behaviors in our lives, through the use of the 165° aspect (or spatial relationship between two planets) known as the "quindecile."

I was greatly comforted, during the process of doing research for this book, to find that I am not alone in having this particular astrological configuration in my natal horoscope. Of the 750 horoscopes examined, I found that 512 of them contained one or more quindecile aspects. Wow! That's a total of 68 percent! This indicates to me, much to my own personal satisfaction, that obsessive-compulsive tendencies are not all that uncommon, and, as a matter of fact, they appear to be present in the majority of people. I strongly believe that the issue here is not whether I, or we, are inclined toward these behaviors, but rather to what degree are they operating in our lives and what is their impact on our overall life development.

During the course of my research, I became aware that when a horoscope contains two or more quindeciles, there is either a sense of cooperation or a strong competitiveness in how they are demonstrated in an individual's life. The quindeciles may echo each other and work together toward reaching a common goal. When this is the case, the influence is less disruptive, and the individual has more ability to utilize this inclination toward a positive end. When this is not the case, the quindeciles may compete with one another and increase the intensity of dis-ease in the individual's life. Understanding how to unify these dynamics toward a beneficial end becomes the first step in the process of positive redirection.

The purpose of this book is first to assist you with understanding the dynamics of obsessive-compulsive tendencies as a human condition; second, to provide information on the viability of using this alignment for benefit rather than hindrance in your life; and third, to introduce the astrological relevance of the quindecile aspect as an indicator of this inclination.

---

1. See *DSM-III-R (Diagnostic and Statistical Manual of Mental Disorders)* (Washington, D.C.: American Psychiatric Association, 1987) 245.

PART I

The Psychology of Obsession

Understanding the dynamics of obsession and compulsion has been a tireless pursuit of mine for many years now, not because of any great work that I wanted to do with other people, but in an attempt to understand the part of my own personality that frequently appears to get out of control. How do I know that it gets out of control? Mostly, because other people tell me it does. Left to my own means, I would stay focused (obsessed) with whatever project I am involved with for days, weeks, or even months at a time. Now, I must tell you, to me this is not a problem, but for those who love and care about me, it very definitely is a problem. They have to sit by and watch me run myself into the ground, again and again, in a continual effort to prove myself to the rest of the world.

In my pursuit of understanding this aspect of my personality, since I do not have a degree in psychology and have never been formally educated in understanding the human psyche, I did the next best thing. I went to work in the mental health and addictions field for many years, spent many years delving into my own psyche with the help of trained professionals, and surrounded myself with family and friends who had the knowledge I so desperately sought. It is the accumulated understanding and realizations gained through these processes that I share with you now.

Obsession is a byproduct of accumulated anxiety. It is the mind's way of focusing itself in order to defend itself against painful emotions connected with trauma or wounds sustained in early development. Compulsion is the action taken to release this accumulated anxiety.

In the clinical diagnosis of obsessive-compulsive disorder, the anxiety that produces obsession is of an ongoing duration, and the compulsion that relieves the anxiety is normally short-lived and must be repeated often. This can be demonstrated in activities such as repetitive hand washing, checking and rechecking lights and locks, and so on. It is not this category of obsessive-compulsive behavior to which I am referring in this book. A disorder of this magnitude must be dealt with by a licensed psychologist or psychiatrist.

For the rest of us, however, who have obsessive-compulsive tendencies and behaviors of a nonclinical nature, there are other forms of help. In this instance, I am referring to behaviors such as codependency, alcoholism, drug abuse, workaholism, shopping, gambling, eating disorders, sexual addictions, perfectionism, idealism, and the use of manipulation and/or control. Consciously working on these issues, perhaps with the aid of a counselor or therapist, helps us gain awareness into our behaviors. This process not only offers us an opportunity to heal those wounded parts of ourselves that influence our actions and reactions, but also allows us the opportunity to redirect those energies, resulting in amazing outcomes.

These behaviors are centered around an attempt to maintain control of our emotional lives. When we unconsciously or subconsciously avoid dealing with our feelings, because of fear and anxiety, we will naturally gravitate toward whatever will offer us relief. Whatever that thought, deed, or action may be, it will provide us with some form of comfort at the time.

One of the benefits experienced during times of obsession is that we are granted a momentary escape from feeling the emotional pain connected with fear, disappointment, anger, low self-esteem, difficult memories, and so on. This escape can become addictive. It can be used like a drug or alcohol, providing us with relief at a moment's notice. It can become our means of coping with the inner stress that perhaps we can't deal with, don't want to deal with, or simply don't have the tools to deal with.

All of us have become obsessive-compulsive at some time about something in our lives. Maybe it was simply about how our hair looked, about always being on time, about cleaning the house, about being available when someone needed us, or about beating the blankety-blank computer at solitaire. These behaviors easily become a part of our normal routine. This is why it is so hard for us to recognize some of these tendencies and behaviors in ourselves. As in my case, it frequently takes an outside observer to point out that there is a problem. What we need to ask ourselves is why this particular behavior is such an important and integral part of our lives. The answer to this will always be that we are fearful or avoiding something else.

Take the situation of a woman who obsesses about how her hair looks every morning before going to work. Society would say that this is appropriate. After all, shouldn't we try to put our best foot forward whenever we go into the work world? Isn't our physical appearance part of how we are judged in that arena? Surely, this woman is only doing her best to feel confident and self-assured. While this may be true, if she is unable to be comfortable with herself simply because her hair isn't perfect, then the issue is more than what it appears to be. This behavior does not seriously challenge the structure of her life. Therefore we must ask, why does perfect hair give her a feeling of self-assurance or confidence that should really come from a healthy self-esteem? It is normal to have a "bad hair day," but when having one affects the function and feeling of how that day will go, then the hair issue is actually a cover-up for a deeper problem.

CHAPTER 1

The Psychological Dynamics of Obsessive-Compulsive Behavior

Life Development Factors
That Influence Obsession and Compulsion

The wounds of early childhood create tears in our emotional structure. These tears create holes, and the more tears we experience, the larger the holes may become. These holes in our emotional structure impact us mentally, physically, and spiritually. We then use behaviors, actions, and attitudes in an attempt to fill the holes so that we no longer feel the pain and emptiness they contain.

Childhood wounding may be the result of abusive parents, dysfunctional families, difficulty with siblings, the death of a loved one, early difficulties in school, incessant teasing or bullying by other young children, moving away from a familiar and secure environment to a new and therefore frightening place . . . the list could go on and on. A good friend of mine once told me that "the severity of a wound that is inflicted is not about the force of the instrument used to wound the individual. It is always about how sensitive the skin is that receives the wound." Therefore the issue of whether or not the wounding was intentional is of less consequence than how the wound was felt by the individual receiving it. The perception of the wound is as real as the wound itself.

For example, if we come from an early environment where we did not receive the amount or kind of nurturing that we felt we needed, it is probable that the obsession and compulsion will manifest in the form of relationship issues. When satisfactory emotional nurturing is not present during early development, it can easily become the focus of adult life. Attaining that which was lacking or absent in childhood can be a primary motivator of behavior. As an adult, even if we become involved in a nurturing relationship, it is possible that we will not recognize it as such because it does not feel familiar. Knowledge, through memory, of how being nurtured feels is not readily available. Therefore, we may not know when or if we have found it. The idea of what nurturing should feel like is very often different from the reality.

Until we take steps to go back into the often distressing reality of what we perceived was missing or painful during our early lives, we will never heal from those wounds. We will continually seek ways to "fill the hole" or bandage the wound because the anxiety surrounding the memories of those times is so uncomfortable. We will be drawn to use whatever reassures and comforts us for the moment, again and again.

If we accept the challenge of doing the work necessary to deal with those parts of our emotional selves that have been damaged, we have the opportunity to heal ourselves. This process then allows for a renewed source of energy that can then be directed and focused into positive, productive parts of our lives.

The Many Ways Obsession and Compulsion Are Demonstrated in Today's Society

In these days of expected and accepted "overdoing," obsessive-compulsive tendencies are continually presented to us as the "norm." The pressure that is present in our current society to "keep up with the Jones" promotes an inner belief that if we don't have the house, car, clothes, body, and lifestyle that we are fed by the advertising world and the media, then there must be something wrong with us. We are constantly bombarded with images of affluence, romance, adventure, and success. We take these images and compare them to the reality of our lives and most often come up feeling that we are lacking in some way. What do we do with these feelings of inadequacy? We try harder, work longer, spend more, and still end up trying to hide away those parts of ourselves that don't fit within that societal image.

The most prominent obsessive-compulsive behavior in society today has to do with body image. As a nation, we focus on the physical body more than any other country in the world. Not only do we spend millions of dollars on diet products and memberships in health clubs, but whatever we can't manage to "fix" ourselves we take to a cosmetic surgeon for a tuck, reduction, lift, or augmentation. Americans have become obsessed with looking young forever and spend a fortune trying to accomplish just that. Our society has little room, or acceptance, for the natural aging process. "Young and fit" has become synonymous with "intelligent and competent."

The second most prominent obsessive-compulsive behavior in our society today is workaholism. This is not just because of the emotional relief found in that particular behavior, but it is also because of the financial pressure under which we live. The cost of our "standard of living" requires at least two incomes in order to live the life that we are told is "normal." After putting eight hours a day into the workplace, we still need to spend time keeping up the home and attempting to maintain a positive family life. The standards by which our society measures us require us to be like Wonder Woman and Superman.

Another rampant example of obsessive-compulsive behavior is the use of drugs and alcohol. This particular behavior is not only widespread, it is almost a mandate within all classes of society. Again, the media bombards us with images of how cool we will be with a "tall, icy cold . . . ," and how irresistible we are to the opposite sex as long as we have a wine spritzer in our hands. Such behavior is now the acceptable way to relax after a hard day's work and is a prerequisite at almost all social gatherings.

Codependency is yet another obsessive-compulsive behavior that has permeated our society. If we can't or don't want to "fix" ourselves, then we need only find another human being to make us okay. Instead of learning how to love and appreciate ourselves, it is far easier to seek affirmation continually through relationships. Then all we have to be is exactly whatever that other person wants us to be, and we will receive from them all that we are unable to give ourselves. This is perhaps the biggest fantasy of all.

We have come to believe that as long as we can function in society, we are okay. Even our insurance companies, when paying for psychological or therapeutic services, now focus on only getting the individual functional enough to get back to work. For the most part, in-depth therapy is a thing of the past. Instead of probing to identify the origin of the problem and healing that part of the psyche, the mandate is to deal with the immediate problem at hand and forget the rest. Consequently, the defenses and manipulations that we have continually used in order to remain functional then become our most treasured possessions.

CHAPTER 2

Obsession and Compulsion as Opportunity versus Difficulty

Redirecting Difficult Behaviors into Potential Positive Manifestation

In my opinion, there is enough energy contained in obsessive-compulsive tendencies to blast off the next space shuttle. It is astounding how much time, energy, and focus we put into these behaviors. They become habit and often do not manifest to the point of obliterating our entire lives, so we continually fall back on them because they are familiar and comforting.

When tendencies, impulses, or behaviors are unconscious, they are driven by a perceived unfulfilled need. Awareness provides us with opportunities to meet that need through many different ways; however, as long as the need remains undefined, alternative solutions also remain undefined. We then have no option but to continue to quiet our anxiety through whatever means we have found to work in the past.

The anxiety produced by unfulfilled needs is somewhat like the "monster in the dark" that scared us at night as a child. Once the lights were turned on, we could see the monster for exactly what it was, and proceed to remove the toy, chair, doll, or whatever else it

was that had created the monster. Magically, the monster then dis-
appeared and we were able to sleep. So, the first step in being able
to redirect obsessive-compulsive tendencies is to identify what unfulfilled need is attached to the anxiety masked by the behavior
being demonstrated.

In my case, my unfulfilled need is about feeling valued. This relates back to early childhood difficulties and massively affects my
self-esteem. This issue disguises itself as a need to prove myself constantly to the rest of the world. This push is then focused into whatever I am working on at the time. In this way I can prove to you that
I am valuable and worthwhile, and then maybe you will love me.
Boy, was that hard to put on paper! When I strip it down to the
bones, the bottom line is an unfulfilled need for self-approval.
Bingo! I now have the necessary information to reduce my anxiety
and subsequently redirect my behavior. Instead of working so hard
to prove myself to you, I need to put the same amount of energy
into feeling good about me. I need to work toward being the person
I want to be, instead of the person I think you want me to be.

When we identify our unfulfilled need, we can then look for
ways to fill that need ourselves. By taking steps (redirecting the energy) to accomplish this, we are being proactive in creating and
maintaining a healthy emotional life. Just keep in mind that if the
steps you take become as obsessive-compulsive as your previous
behavior, then you are probably trapped back in old habits. Stop,
look at your behavior, and be open to talking about it with others.
Then begin working with these principles again.

PART II

An Astrological Overview
of the Quindecile

When interpreting the horoscope, there are many factors that must be taken into account before a specific judgment or supposition should be made. The use of the quindecile, as a reference of obsessive-compulsive tendency, is only one of these factors. When analyzing a horoscope, we must understand it within the context of that individual's life. The formation of personality and individuation through psychological development is not defined solely by the planetary positions at the time of birth. The horoscope is only an indication of possibility and probability. There are many other factors that can, and will, influence how an individual responds and integrates the particular combination of planetary energies present at the time of his or her birth.

Life development is determined by many different factors. There is socioeconomic environment, parental influence and relationship, level of education, place of birth, and era or time into which one is born, to name but a few. If we look only at the information contained in the horoscope and do not take into account these other developmental influences, we quickly fall into the trap of making snap judgments that may not fit the individual's reality. It is essential, when dealing with the psychological nature of the horoscope, that we interpret the planetary dynamics that are suggested in the scope of reality present in that individual's life.

The horoscope examples detailed in this book are intended to show not only difficult or problematic manifestations of obsessive and compulsive tendencies, but also positive and productive manifestation possibilities.

CHAPTER 3

The History of the Quindecile

The quindecile, or 165° aspect, was first brought into astrological awareness by German astrologer Thomas Ring (1892–1983). He utilized it in his work on the horoscope of Leonardo da Vinci, noting it in the relationship of Leonardo's Moon in Pisces (the emotional need to merge sensitivity, intuitiveness, and working with the intangible) and Neptune in Libra (seeking the illusive, imaginary, and ideal through all to which it relates). Thomas Ring termed this 165° spacial relationship "the separation aspect," denoting its characteristics to be those of disruption and upheaval that divorce the individual from the balance of his or her life, through the nature of the two planets involved.

The use of this aspect then faded into the background of astrology until it was rediscovered by international astrologer Noel Tyl, who came across the work done by Thomas Ring while researching the horoscope of Leonardo da Vinci for his book *Astrology of the Famed*. Noel Tyl did extensive research, through the use of over 600 horoscopes, and confirmed it to be a most prominent indicator of upheaval and separation in an individual's life. Mr. Tyl included in his work the concept of obsession-compulsion as a factor in the manifestation of this aspect, denoting it as a response to upset and trauma in one's life.

Understanding of the 165° relationship between planets is now being introduced to astrologers all over the world through the work done by Noel Tyl and enthusiasts such as myself, who have begun to work with and continue to research this aspect.

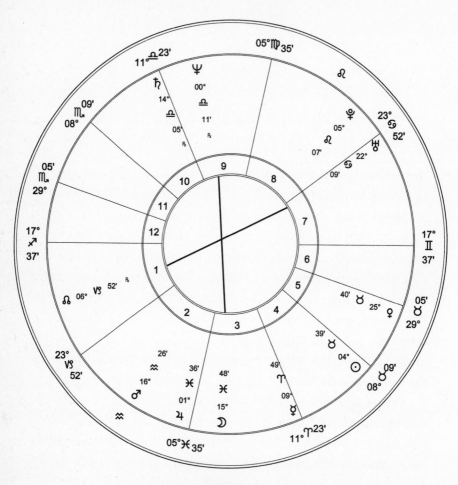

Horoscope 1
Leonardo da Vinci / April 15, 1452 / Vinci, Italy / 10:30 P.M. LMT
(Rectification by Noel Tyl. See Noel Tyl, *Astrology of the Famed*, St. Paul, MN: Llewellyn Publications, 1996, page 240.)

Leonardo da Vinci, perhaps one of the most renowned and beloved artists of all time, is acclaimed for his artistic sensitivity and depth of detailed perfection in his work. It is well-known and documented that Leonardo relentlessly pursued perfection and universal understanding that was not only focused in his artistic endeavors, but found its way into all facets of his life. He is known to have been extremely generous, noble, and kind, with an intelligence that appeared to know no bounds. His mind was always seeking a higher understanding of not only the artistic and creative realms with which he worked, but also the physical world around him. He studied everything from anatomy, mechanics, and aerodynamics, to the animals and plants he encountered in his immediate environment. He was an innovator of thought and an inventor of things far beyond their time.

Despite the incredibly perceptive, technical, and precise mind that Leonardo possessed, he appeared to be unable to finalize many of the tasks set before him. Most of his artistic works were never completed, and much of his inventive genius never got beyond the detailed descriptions written in the multitude of journals he religiously kept throughout his lifetime.

Leonardo had a penchant for writing everything in meticulous detail. He not only recorded his ideas and observations, but also made itemized grocery lists and kept accountings of each and every purchase. In all his journals there is a glaring deficiency in the writing of anything about himself. There is no mention of what or how he felt, nor any notation in reference to himself or how he personally related to others or to the world around him.

There are two quindeciles in Leonardo da Vinci's natal horoscope that shed some light on his enigmatic yet fascinating life. The obsessive-compulsive push of his sensitive artistic expression can easily be seen in his well-known paintings of the *Mona Lisa* and *The Last Supper*. Leonardo's Neptune in Libra (seeking the illusive, imaginary, and ideal through all to which it relates) was quindecile his Moon in Pisces (the emotional need to utilize sensitivity, intuitiveness, and working with the intangible). The incredible gift of artistic creativity that this combination provides is enormous and shows itself through the sensitivity of Leonardo's paintings. This particular combination also makes it almost impossible for the reality of what is manifested to ever live up to the idealized dream. How painful it must have been for Leonardo to realize, with each and every artistic endeavor, that perfection itself is always in the eye of the beholder, when Leonardo's own eye must have always seen that there was more to be done.

The intense thirst of Leonardo's creative mind is seen easily in the many technical drawings and calibrated calculations for numerous machines and inventions contained in his journals. Leonardo's Uranus in Cancer (disruption of the status quo through unique and innovative ideas in work for the family and the people) was quindecile his North Node in Capricorn (a calling forth of the life purpose through hard work, ambition, and goals). Again, how painful it must have been to know that all things are possible through advancement of technology, yet be unable to bring those concepts into reality.

That same Uranus in Cancer (disruption of the status quo through the family) quindecile the North Node in Capricorn (the maternal influence within ambition and goals) also suggests a separation from the mother during early life, as was the case with Leonardo. Some even propose that the *Mona Lisa* is actually a portrait of Leonardo's mother.

CHAPTER 4

Technical Information About the Quindecile

Identifying the Quindecile in a Chart

Since the quindecile is a 165° aspect and the opposition is a 180° aspect dividing the zodiacal circle in half, it is easy to locate the quindecile 15° from either side of the opposition point (180° − 165° = 15°). Keep in mind that we are dealing with a continuous circle, and therefore it does not matter from which direction the 165° is measured. This aspect is easy to sightsee by finding the opposition point of any given planet in the horoscope, and then adding or subtracting 15° to or from that opposition point.

Examples:

15° Aries–Quindecile point = 0° Scorpio or 0° Libra.

    The opposition point (180°) for 15° Aries is 15° Libra. If we add 15° to 15° Libra, we arrive at 30° Libra/0° Scorpio. If we subtract 15° from 15° Libra, we arrive at 0° Libra.

2° Gemini–Quindecile point = 17° Sagittarius or 17° Scorpio.

    The opposition point (180°) for 2° Gemini is 2° Sagittarius. If we add 15° to 2° Sagittarius, we arrive at 17° Sagittarius. If we subtract 15° from 2° of Sagittarius (take 2° away to arrive at 0°

Sagittarius and continue back another 13° into the sign of Scorpio), we arrive at 17° Scorpio (30° – 13° = 17°).

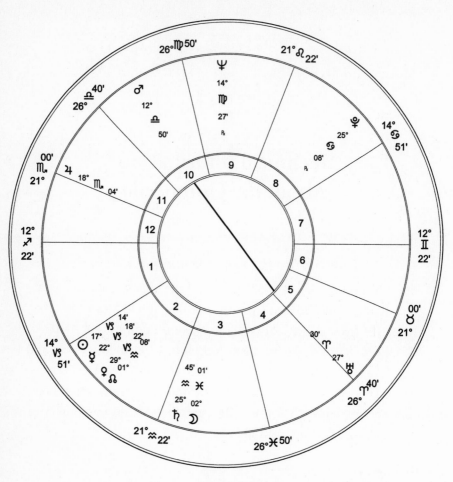

Horoscope 2
Elvis Presley / January 8, 1935 / Tupelo, MS / 4:35 A.M. CST

Elvis Presley has Uranus at 27° Aries (located in the fifth house) quindecile Mars at 12° Libra (located in the eleventh house).

The opposition point of Mars at 12° Libra is 12° Aries. If we add 15° to that opposition point, we arrive at 27° Libra, which is also the position of Uranus.

The opposition point of Uranus at 27° Aries is 27° Libra. If we subtract 15° from that opposition point, we arrive at 12° Libra, which is also the position of Mars.

Understanding the 24th-Harmonic Aspect

The use of the word "harmonic" relates to the tone or vibratory level of any number of parts divided equally into a common area. In Western astrology, we work with the 360° circle of the zodiac. Therefore, within this reference, a second-harmonic aspect would relate to the division of the circle equally by two with each section being 180° (180° x 2 = 360°), a third-harmonic aspect would relate to the division of the circle equally by three with each section being 120° (120° x 3 = 360°), a fourth-harmonic aspect would relate to the division of the circle equally by four with each section being 90° (90° x 4 = 360°), and so on.

The 24th harmonic would then relate to the division of the circle equally by twenty-four with each section being 15° (15° x 24 = 360°). It is interesting to note that in modern-day astrology, there are already aspects (within orb allowance) assigned to each of the accumulated 15° divisions of the zodiacal circle, with the exception of the initial 15° placement and the 165° placement.

0°	Conjunction	30°	Semisextile
45°	Semisquare	60°	Sextile
72°	Quintile (3° orb)	90°	Square
102°	Biseptile (3° orb)	120°	Trine
135°	Sesquiquadrate	150°	Quincunx
180°	Opposition		

The word "quindecile" is Latin for the word "fifteen." Therefore the use of the word "quindecile," as it relates to an aspect, infers that it is a division or divisions of the circle by equal parts of 15° increments, bringing us back to the 24th harmonic (15° x 24 = 360°).

Since ten of the twelve 15° incremental possibilities are already assigned to specific aspects, it would make logical sense that the remaining two placements, at 15° and 165°, would indicate aspectual relevance within astrological understanding.

It is the 24th-harmonic placement that we are concerned with in this book, and it is this 165° placement that has been named the "quindecile."

Orbs

All astrologers have their own opinions and rules regarding the amount of orb to allow for any given planetary relationship. I, myself, like to keep orbs very small (or "tight," as they are referred to in astrology). When synthesizing the various components of a horoscope, I like to focus on things that are of major impact in the individual's life. Wide or large orbs tend to give *more* information, but with less specific focus on the dynamics of the individual's life.

Natal

In the natal or birth horoscope, I normally allow up to a 2° orb (either side of exact) for all planets, with the exception of the Sun and Moon. Because of the importance of the Sun and Moon, I may extend my normal orb allowance and use up to a 2½° orb with these particular luminaries. It is only in cases of horoscopes that have minimal or no tension aspects that I will exceed these maximum orbs. In the rare cases when this happens, I will only increase the orb allowance to 3° for the Sun and Moon, and 2½° for all other planets. Despite the fact that the quindecile has major meaning and manifestation potential in the development and focus of one's life, it is still classified as a minor aspect. It should, therefore, be utilized only with minimal orb allowances.

Progressions

When incorporating planets that are making an aspect by progression (whether secondary progressions or solar arc directions) into the natal horoscope, I work only with a 1° orb allowance. The actual time frame involved, when a progressed planet comes into alignment with a natal planet, is an important factor to consider. Therefore, I only synthesize progressed planetary alignments once they have moved to within 1° of the natal planet being aspected.

Intense periods of manifestation, created by progressed planets in alignment with natal planets, are demonstrated at the time when the aspect is exact. However, my research has shown that awareness of the issues involved may not be recognized until after the progressed planet has begun to separate from the exact position. Therefore, I continue to work with this aspect until it has moved out of alignment by 1°. The build-up to becoming an exact progressed aspect is normally a time of increasing intensity, while the movement away from the exact position may be the time of making necessary changes. Often we do not let go of, or wish to redirect, a particular tendency or behavior until full awareness of the effects has been realized.

For instance, if Mars is at 9° Taurus in the natal horoscope, I would only consider a progressed second planet to be quindecile to Mars when it reaches 23°, 24°, and 25° Scorpio or Libra. This is because the opposition point of Mars at 9° Taurus is 9° Scorpio. When we add or subtract 15°, we arrive at 24° Scorpio or Libra. Thus, 1° approaching the exact position would be 23°, the exact position would be 24°, and 1° separating from the exact position would be 25° Scorpio or Libra.

Transits

When incorporating aspects created through alignment of transiting planets to natal planets, the amount of orb to be utilized is a little more complicated. The differing rates of speed at which the planets travel through our solar system impact the time frame of alignment. Some of the transiting planets will be in aspect to a natal planet for only a few hours or days, while others will remain aspectually aligned for months or even a year or two. Because of this differing planetary movement, I have found that it is important to allow a wider orb for the faster personal planets and a smaller orb for the slower societal and generational planets. In reality, unless I am looking for information relating to a short period of time (i.e., a day, week, or month), I rarely utilize the transiting personal planets as a means of information. My focus normally begins with Jupiter and Saturn, allowing a 2° orb, followed by Uranus, Neptune, and Pluto, where I allow only a 1° orb.

Synastry

When working with synastry (relationship) horoscopes, I utilize the same rules I use for individual natal horoscopes. This is normally a 2° orb for all planets, with the exception of the Sun and Moon for which I may allow a 2½° orb. I have found that relationships appearing to have an obsessive-compulsive component most often contain quindecile alignment(s) between planets from one horoscope to the other.

CHAPTER 5

Dynamics of Analysis of the Quindecile

Understanding the Placement of 165°

The 165° point, within the natural zodiacal circle, falls at 15° Virgo and again at 15° Libra. Since the nature of Virgo is all about assimilation and the nature of Libra is all about cooperation, I believe that the higher purpose of the quindecile is about effectively assimilating a cooperative effort of the planetary pair's characteristics into one's life.

The elements of earth (Virgo) and air (Libra) suggest that the dynamics of the quindecile will be involved in combining the physical and mental realms together in one's life. In other words, "Do what you think!" Virgo is a mutable (flexible) sign, and Libra is a cardinal (active) sign, further indicating that this particular aspect will have an active component that may go around in circles. When these dynamics are not consciously focused, chaos and disruption reign in one's life through the characteristics of the two planets involved.

The quindecile falls at the midpoint between a quincunx (150°) and an opposition (180°). This indicates a coming together of adjustment (quincunx) and awareness (opposition). Through a process of awareness combined with a conscious effort to adjust and modify the energies involved, we are provided with an opportunity to utilize this dynamic to our benefit.

Delineation Differences

In order for us to understand how any particular astrological alignment may manifest, we must take into account the sign, house, and aspects in which each of the planets are placed. The combination of all the components of this equation influence exactly how those planets will work together and manifest in one's life.

The purpose of this book is not to educate the reader about signs, elements, quadriplicities, aspects, houses, and so on. However, it will be helpful to the newcomer to at least have a basic concept of what the possible combinations may suggest.

Element Combinations

The signs of the zodiac reference the "how" of life. They are suggestive of the manner in which the manifestation of energy displays itself. All signs of the zodiac are contained in the four basic elements of fire, earth, air, and water, with three signs per element. The element to which a sign belongs is the first key to understanding how a planet may express itself in that sign. For instance, a planet in a water sign seeks to manifest itself in terms of emotional expression. If we are looking at a planet in an earth sign, it may seek to express itself in a practical or physical-world manner. In the case of a planet in an air sign, we need to look toward the social responses of communication, mental comprehension, and intellectual pursuits. Last but not least, if we are seeking to understand the dynamics of a planet placed in a fire sign, we must look at it through the eyes of passion, energy, and inspiration.

The Elements

Fire & Earth

Aries/Virgo, Leo/Capricorn, Sagittarius/Taurus.
The heat of passion linked to physical-world reality.

Fire & Air
Aries/Libra, Leo/Aquarius, Sagittarius/Gemini.
The heat of passion linked to social exchange.

Fire & Water
Aries/Scorpio, Leo/Pisces, Sagittarius/Cancer.
The heat of passion linked to emotional responses.

Earth & Air
Taurus/Libra, Virgo/Aquarius, Capricorn/Gemini.
Physical-world reality linked to social exchange.

Earth & Water
Taurus/Scorpio, Virgo/Pisces, Capricorn/Cancer.
Physical-world reality linked to emotional responses.

Air & Water
Gemini/Scorpio, Libra/Pisces, Aquarius/Cancer.
Social exchange linked to emotional responses.

Modality Combinations

Within the assigned elemental groupings of the zodiac, there are also subsections (modalities). These modalities provide additional clues as to the nature of any particular sign's manner of expression. Within each element there are three zodiacal signs, creating three modality subsections. These modalities are known as cardinal, fixed, and mutable. The cardinal modality focuses on initiation of energy and action, the fixed modality focuses on maintaining and sustaining, and the mutable modality focuses on adjusting and changing.

The Modalities

Cardinal & Cardinal
Aries/Libra, Cancer/Capricorn.
React and respond.

Cardinal & Fixed

Aries/Scorpio, Cancer/Aquarius, Libra/Taurus, Capricorn/Leo.
React and resist.

Cardinal & Mutable

Aries/Virgo, Cancer/Sagittarius, Libra/Pisces, Capricorn/Gemini.
React and revise.

Fixed & Fixed

Taurus/Scorpio, Leo/Aquarius.
Resist and retain.

Fixed & Mutable

Taurus/Sagittarius, Leo/Pisces, Scorpio/Gemini, Aquarius/Virgo.
Resist and revise.

Mutable & Mutable

Gemini/Sagittarius, Virgo/Pisces.
Revise and refine.

The Sign Possibilities by Both Element and Modality

Signs • Elements • Modalities

Aries/Virgo • Fire & Earth • Cardinal & Mutable

Heat of passion linked to physical world. Reacts and refines.

This combination is project-oriented. May start too many projects at the same time, thus having a difficult time finishing any one thing. Positive focus through targeting goals toward constant improvement.

H. G. Wells, Rudolph Nureyev, B. F. Skinner, Dustin Hoffman

Aries/Libra • Fire & Air • Cardinal & Cardinal

Heat of passion linked to social exchange. Reacts and responds.

Seeks reaction and recognition from others. The act of interaction drives this combination. Relationship needs, public persona.

Needs to be affirmed and appreciated by others. Positive focus through awareness and action in relation to other's needs.
Jim Jones, Elvis Presley, Jerry Garcia, Heinrich Himmler

Aries/Scorpio • Fire & Water • Cardinal & Fixed
Heat of passion linked to emotional response. Reacts and retains.

Driven by intensity of feelings. The "heat of the moment" feeds this combination. Passionate, argumentative, and sexual. Tries to control through initiating action. Positive focus through actively transforming and reforming psychological basis.
Marlon Brando, Lauren Bacall, Luciano Pavarotti, Joan Crawford

Taurus/Libra • Earth & Air • Fixed & Cardinal
Physical-world reality linked to social exchange. Resists and reacts.

Has a hard time letting go of people and things. Actively pushes for security through material possessions and relationships. Value of self measured through others. Positive focus through providing benefit for others.
Prince Charles, Shirley MacLaine, Giorgio Armani, Linda Lovelace

Taurus/Scorpio • Earth & Water • Fixed & Fixed
Physical-world reality linked to emotional response. Resists and retains.

Material possessions equal security. Driven by fears of emotional and/or physical loss. Works hard. Is dogmatic and resistant to change. May attempt to control purse strings. Difficulty in making changes and letting go. Positive focus through the value of self-evaluation.
Coco Chanel, Fred Astaire, Marilyn Monroe, Madonna

Taurus/Sagittarius • Earth & Fire • Fixed & Mutable
Physical-world reality linked to heat of passion. Resists and refines.

Long-range planner. Pragmatic. Holds philosophical and/or religious opinions. Difficulty letting go of ideas and concepts. Follows a purpose or "calling" forcefully. Positive focus through structured education and the setting of goals through a practical, tangible, common-sense approach.

Winston Churchill, Karl Marx, George H. Bush, Jackie Robinson

Gemini/Scorpio • Air & Water • Mutable & Fixed
Social exchange linked to emotional response. Revises and retains.

Intense mental acuity. Verbal and mental manipulation. Difficulty in letting go of ideas.

Can present information or ideas as different, but they still remain the same. Plots and schemes. Positive focus through communication and understanding of psychological basis.

O. J. Simpson, Carry Nation, Lucky Luciano, Oprah Winfrey

Gemini/Sagittarius • Air & Fire • Mutable & Mutable
Social exchange linked to heat of passion. Revises and refines.

Belief systems taken to the maximum. Opinions and ideas are plentiful. May never shut up. Excellent brainstormer and problem solver, but has difficulty implementing ideas. Positive focus through educational expansion.

Paul Joseph Goebbels, Nicolas Copernicus, Karl Marx,
Paramahansa Yogananda

Gemini/Capricorn • Air & Earth • Mutable & Cardinal
Social exchange linked to physical-world reality.
Revises and responds.

"Climbs the ladder" through the use of social contacts. Takes the lead and authority position through communication. Pushes concepts into reality. Can focus on the negative and have problems with depression. Positive focus in setting goals and strategic planning. Options present opportunities.

Emmaline Pankhurst, Barbra Streisand, Louis Pasteur, Joan of Arc

Cancer/Sagittarius • Water & Fire • Cardinal & Mutable
Emotional response linked to heat of passion. Reacts and refines.

Runs "hot and cold." Seeks emotional security here, there, and everywhere. Can suffocate others with excessive nurturing and exaggerated feelings. Can play the role of "the drama queen/king." Positive focus through teaching others.
Liberace, Janis Joplin, Frank Sinatra, Ernest Hemingway

Cancer/Capricorn • Water & Earth • Cardinal & Cardinal
Emotional response linked to physical-world reality.
Reacts and responds.

Security tied to success. Pursuit of ambitions creates feeling of safety. Must constantly push to prove self. Responsibility is pursued. Expresses through doing, not through feeling. Positive focus through active involvement with family.
Jane Fonda, Jimmy Hoffa, John F. Kennedy, Sean Connery

Cancer/Aquarius • Water & Air • Cardinal & Fixed
Emotional response linked to social exchange. Reacts and retains.

Gets caught in social reform, creative enterprises, and the welfare of humankind. "Mothers" the world. Fights tirelessly for the underdog. Ideas become issues. Positive focus through fun with family and friends.
Ralph Nader, Franklin D. Roosevelt, Oral Roberts, Shirley MacLaine

Leo/Capricorn • Fire & Earth • Fixed & Cardinal
Heat of passion linked to physical-world reality.
Resists and responds.

Pursues achievement and ambition with determination. Seeks to be recognized, respected, and honored. Pushes forward to success for ego gratification. Can be ruthless in application. Positive focus through sharing responsibility and giving recognition to others.
Napoleon I, Henry VIII, Margaret Thatcher, Merv Griffin

Leo/Aquarius • Fire & Air • Fixed & Fixed
Heat of passion linked to social exchange. Resists and retains.

Stubborn within the "fight" for acknowledgment of being right. The rules apply to everyone else, "just not to me because I know a better way." Relationships extremely intense. Rebels for recognition. Difficulty letting go of others. Needs a "cause." Positive focus through charitable works.

George Wallace, Brigham Young, Ted Kennedy, Lucille Ball

Leo/Pisces • Fire & Water • Fixed & Mutable
Heat of passion linked to emotional response. Resists and refines.

Idealized perceptions of importance. Dreams and fantasy of recognition outweigh practical application. Can martyr self to gain focus of attention. Pursues desires zealously, then gives up or changes course. Positive focus through dedication to artistic and creative endeavors or focusing the goals into the realm of physical possibility.

Amy Fisher, Mata Hari, Isadora Duncan, Ivana Trump

Virgo/Aquarius • Earth & Air • Mutable & Fixed
Physical-world reality linked to social exchange.
Revises and retains.

Disrupts the "status quo" with innovative concepts and ideas. Changes systems without regard to possible consequences. Seeks to do the "greater good" through constant improvement. Positive manifestation through technological orientation.

Timothy Leary, Marlene Dietrich, Chevy Chase, Richard Chamberlain

Virgo/Pisces • Earth & Water • Mutable & Mutable
Physical-world reality linked to emotional response.
Revises and refines.

Behavior dependent upon feelings. Hypochondria, health, and physical problems can be issues. Escapism and physical addictions prominent. The workaholic. May play the martyr. Positive focus

through spiritual understanding and working with the intuitive and intangible.
Woody Allen, Jack Kerouac, Dave Brubeck, Quincy Jones

Libra/Pisces • **Air & Water** • **Cardinal & Mutable**
Social exchange linked to emotional response. Reacts and refines.

Seeks to understand self through others. Idealization of relationships, codependency, and relationship addictions prominent. The perception of ideal may always be better than the physical reality. Pursues whatever others pursue. "Joins the club." Positive focus through taking action developing a relationship with the self and a spiritual source.
Leonardo da Vinci, Sigmund Freud, Dr. Norman Vincent Peale, Doris Day

Expression of the Quindecile Aspect

The overall manner in which a quindecile may be expressed is determined by the specific nature of the individual planets and angles that are involved. We must take into account the focus and importance of those particular planets and angles, in addition to other aspectual relationships they may be making, and how this all fits in the horoscope as a whole.

Planets in quindecile aspect to the angles show themselves outwardly to others. The characteristics of these particular planets are "on display" for the world to see.

Personal planets in quindecile aspect to other personal planets are incorporated more into the general personality. The characteristics of each planetary "leg" are blended into a singular dynamic through which the obsessive-compulsive tendencies are channeled.

When personal planets are in quindecile aspect to societal planets, this indicates an opportunity to take a position or stand within the defining of trends and fashions of society at that particular time.

When outer planets are in quindecile aspect to other outer planets, this is part of the evolutionary cycle of our societies and humankind in general. People born at these times may be part of this process.

The horoscopes contained in this book provide insight into both the negative possibilities of this aspect and also the use of this planetary relationship to encourage us to attempt to reach our positive potentials.

Planet Quindecile the Angles

When a particular planet is quindecile one of the angles of the horoscope, it will be visibly shown by the individual through his or her physical presentation, social outreach, relationships, societal position, or professional endeavors. There is an obsessive-compulsive push forward, expressed through the nature and characteristics of the planet involved, which may dominate what is seen and noted by others. The dynamics of that planet are exhibited through the manner in which the individual approaches and deals with the rest of the world.

Planet Quindecile the Ascendant

A planet quindecile the Ascendant will be shown through the outer personality of the individual. There may be an obsessive-compulsive tendency with reference to the individual's looks, physical body, or relationships. You will see the characteristics of the particular planet aspecting the Ascendant clearly defined by the way the individual presents himself or herself to others and to the world in general.

> *Joan Crawford,* legendary film star of the 1930s and 1940s, had the planet Venus in Aries quindecile her Scorpio Ascendant (self-focused use of aesthetics and kinship to control transformation of personality).

Charles Manson, leader of the cult group in the 1960s that savagely murdered several people, has his Sun in Scorpio quindecile his Taurus Ascendant (recognition of control sought through tangible means).

Amy Fisher, the young girl who had an affair with a married man and decided to kill his wife so they could be together, has her Moon in Libra quindecile her Aries Ascendant (emotional need to be in relationship through personal and self-focused means).

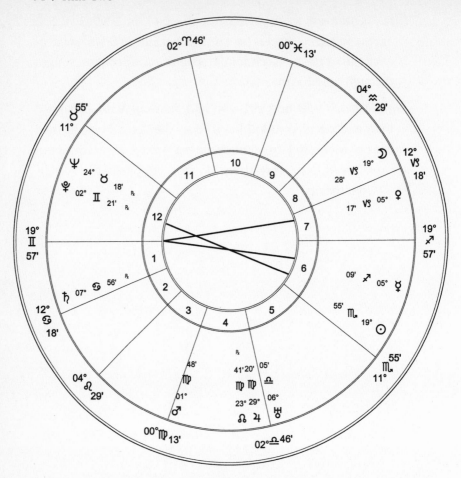

Horoscope 3
General George S. Patton, Jr. / November 11, 1885 / San Marino, CA /
6:36 P.M. PST

General George S. Patton, Jr., was a great tactition and practitioner
of mobile tank warfare during World War II. His men affectionately
referred to him as "Old Blood and Guts." Patton not only was the
consummate soldier, he also looked every bit the part. He wore his
uniform proudly, adorned with symbols of authority, and was
never seen with so much as a wrinkle or a crease out of place. His
attire was part of his ego personification, a symbol of prestige, and
an example of what he expected a soldier to be.

Patton was an excellent troop commander with an ability to rouse his men through speeches of duty and glory. His speeches were rife with profanity and graphic, bloody detail. Despite being instrumental in winning World War II, he was never promoted above the rank of four-star general. The primary barrier to continued advancement and honor in the military was his inability to keep his mouth shut and his opinions to himself. He was overheard on several occasions making loud and inappropriate criticisms to lower-ranking soldiers. He was also noted for his tirades and for pushing his own battle plans, strategic ideas, and personal perspectives into the forefront, regardless of political fallout.

As a child, Patton was dyslexic, with no formal education until the age of eleven. Despite these difficulties, he finished high school, attended Virginia Military Institute, and graduated from West Point. He was a voracious reader, especially of military history, and could memorize large passages from books. He was fluent in several languages, including French and Latin.

When participating in the 1912 Olympic Games, Patton put forth such an extraordinary effort in the swimming competition that he had to be retrieved from the water with the aid of a boat hook at the end of the race. He had three quindeciles in his natal horoscope, two of which involved his Ascendant. His obsessive-compulsive push to be noticed by others and by the world can easily be seen through the thrust of his career and the manner in which he communicated.

His Mercury in Sagittarius (communication of philosophies and belief systems) was quindecile his Ascendant (the outer personality) in Gemini (through ideas and information). Here is his unshakable belief that he could accomplish whatever he thought was needed, whether it be his educational pursuits or his ability to plan the "right" battle strategies. It also contributed to his outbursts, which were lacking in tact and forethought. This particular quindecile is opinionated and loaded with bias because of the

Sagittarian influence and a tendency for Mercury in this particular sign to "shoot off its mouth."

Compounding this was Patton's Venus in Capricorn (aesthetics and kinship within ambition and goals) quindecile that same Gemini Ascendant. Here we have the "commander in chief" projected through his physical appearance—his uniform finely decked out with all his ribbons and medals reinforcing a position of authority, while communicating his values of hard work and cooperation.

In addition, Patton's Pluto in Gemini (empowerment or disempowerment through ideas and information) was quindecile his Sun in Scorpio (recognition sought through control). While this gave added strength to his ability to communicate forcefully and passionately, it also contributed to the perception held by others of an overblown ego. This was compounded by an overpowering compulsion to speak those same values, even at inappropriate times, which ultimately curtailed his advancement in the army he loved so dearly.

Planet Quindecile the Midheaven

A planet quindecile the Midheaven will primarily be noted through the interaction of the individual's ambition and projection to the outside world. It is shown in the external focus of the individual, perhaps through one's career or how the person seeks to be known by society as a whole. The thrust here is for authoritative recognition or approval. The use of the planetary characteristics involved will be a prime part of the individual's push to be acknowledged by others in prominent positions, as well as to attain his or her own position of prominence.

> *Napoleon I,* French ruler and conqueror, had his Moon in Capricorn quindecile his Midheaven in Leo (the emotional need to achieve ambitions and goals within the career or societal position).

Emmaline Pankhurst, leader of the suffragette movement, who led demonstrations and chained herself to railings in protest of women not having the right to vote, had her Uranus in Gemini quindecile her Capricorn Midheaven (disruption of the "status quo" through innovative ambitions and goals within a societal position).

Marla Maples, second wife of Donald Trump, who literally had no "claim to fame" until her affair and subsequent marriage to "The Donald," has her Jupiter in Aries quindecile her Libra Midheaven (exaggerated self-focus through relationship and societal position).

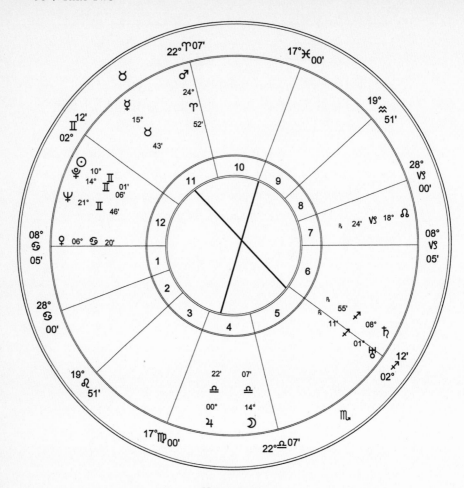

Horoscope 4
Dr. Norman Vincent Peale / May 31, 1898 / Bowersville, OH /
6:11 A.M. CST

Dr. Norman Vincent Peale was one of the most well-known religious leaders, writers, and television personalities of his time. He grew up helping support his family by delivering newspapers, working in a grocery store, and selling pots and pans door to door. He focused on the benefit of hard work combined with love, family unity, and faith in God. He was ordained a Methodist Episcopal minister in 1922, and established a spiritually based psychiatric clinic as part of his ministry in 1937. He authored over twenty-five books including the best-selling *The Art of Loving* (1948), *The Power of Positive Thinking* (1952), and *The Tough-Minded Optimist* (1962). He was an influential lecturer, radio broadcaster, syndicated newspaper columnist, and host of the television program *What's Your Problem?*

Dr. Norman Vincent Peale was renowned for his optimistic outlook and his belief in the benefit of positive mental projection. His philosophy was based on the belief that "you create what you think," and his message was heard and received enthusiastically by millions of people. He applied Christianity to everyday problems and had a keen understanding of human psychology.

The obsessive-compulsive thrust of his beliefs and philosophies is seen throughout his writings and his works as a minister. His Jupiter in Libra (excess within all to which it relates) was quindecile his Pisces Midheaven (sensitivity, intuitiveness, and working with the intangible focused through career and societal position). This particular quindecile served him well, through his focus on the use of spiritual concepts, in becoming a recognizable force for the benefit and betterment of humankind. The same quindecile, however, could potentially manifest as a strong pull toward addictions, use of deceit in the career, and excessive fantasy, along with an inability to produce anything of a practical or physical nature.

Peale's Uranus in Sagittarius (disruption of the status quo through innovative philosophies and belief systems) was quindecile his Mercury in Taurus (communication through tangible means). This is clearly seen through his ability to understand and communicate the problems of common people in a way that could be understood by anyone, despite his combined psychological and spiritual approach.

Planet Quindecile the Sun and Moon

When a planet is quindecile the Sun or Moon, it becomes an integral part of the individual's personality. It is difficult for the individual to see the extent to which the drive of the aspecting planet is influencing the totality of his or her life. Frequently, it takes some kind of outside intervention process for the individual to recognize the need for change. Planets quindecile the Sun or Moon remind me of Siamese twins. Despite their individual natures, they are fused together into one being. Separation is desirable, but also traumatic and complex.

The Sun

Quindeciles to the Sun are demonstrated through the ego. The characteristics of the aspecting planet are incorporated into how the individual seeks recognition, acceptance, and honor from others. Frequently, the drive from the aspecting planet can become offensive and irritating to others because of the intensity with which it pushes to be noticed and received.

> *Winston Churchill,* former prime minister of England whose controlling personality and rousing speeches not only led Britain to victory during World War II but also offended those in positions of power after the war was over, had his Pluto in Taurus quindecile his Sun in Sagittarius (recognition of beliefs and philosophies sought through tangible and powerful perspectives).

> *Quincy Jones,* a brilliant musician, producer of music, and promoter of other musically talented and gifted individuals, has his Neptune in Virgo quindecile his Sun in Pisces (recognition of sensitivity sought through discernment and assimilation of the ideal).

Joan Baez, folk singer of the 1960s who led a generation of people to an understanding of human rights through her soft, lyrical music, has her Pluto in Leo quindecile her Sun in Capricorn (recognition of career and societal position sought through powerful perspectives within creative self-expression).

It is important to note that because of the close proximity of Mercury and Venus to the Sun's orbit, it is not possible for these two planets to ever be in quindecile aspect to the Sun. Mercury never travels more than 28° away from the Sun, and Venus never travels more than 46° from the Sun. Also of note is the fact that Mercury and Venus can never be in quindecile aspect with each other because of their close orbital path.

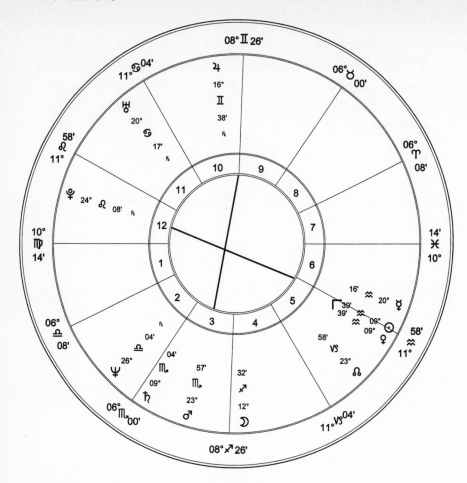

Horoscope 5
Oprah Winfrey / January 29, 1954 / Kosciusko, MS / 7:50 P.M. CST

Oprah Winfrey surely must be the reigning monarch of today's media, but how did she get there? What was the push that drove her to such superstardom?

Oprah was born illegitimate and raised on her grandmother's farm in the deep South. She was sexually molested during her pre-teen years by male relatives, and gave birth to a premature baby at the age of fourteen. She spent much of her teenage years in and out of trouble until she went to Nashville to live with her father, who was a strict disciplinarian. Under his strong influence, with an emphasis on the value of education, Oprah turned her life around. Without a doubt, she is a living symbol of the "self-made" person, despite all odds.

Oprah landed her first broadcasting job at the age of nineteen and went on to study speech and the performing arts at Tennessee State University. From there she began her slow but steady climb to the top, one step at a time. Today she is one of America's most recognizable people, owns her own production company, and is rapidly becoming this country's first black billionaire. She is the benefactress of many charities and not only shares herself with her viewers, but shares her good fortune with those who are less fortunate.

Oprah's Pluto in Leo (empowerment or disempowerment through creative self-expression) is quindecile her Sun in Aquarius (recognition sought through doing something significant, unusual, and different). This gave her the obsessive-compulsive push needed to "put herself out" for all the world to see. It also provided her with a powerhouse of energy and determination to "stay the course." Her Pluto is also quindecile her Venus in Aquarius (kinship and collaboration through doing something significant, unusual, and different), providing her with a forceful need to do something that would be shared with others.

Likewise, her Mars in Scorpio (controlled or transformative action) is quindecile her Gemini Midheaven (ideas and information focused through career and societal position). This is the driving force she displays in her career utilizing transformative ideas. The media provides a perfect venue in which to focus all that energy contained in her Midheaven.

The Moon

Quindeciles to the Moon tend to be less visible to the outsider and more ingrained in the individual's response when security needs are not met. The dynamics involved are much more subtle and hidden in the individual's personality. Once the need for food, water, and shelter have been met, the need for emotional security, as shown through the position of the Moon, is every individual's primary motivation. A quindecile to the Moon intensifies the security needs, and when frustrated in getting those specific needs met, it provides an alternate route to satisfaction. Frequently, the character of the aspecting planet becomes the conscious focus of the obsession-compulsion. However, the true motivation and driving need for security comes from the position of the Moon and not the position of the planet that is making the quindecile aspect.

Timothy Leary, Harvard mathematics professor who in the 1960s promoted the use of LSD and "turned on" a generation of "hippies," has his Jupiter in Virgo quindecile his Moon in Aquarius (the emotional need to do something significant, unusual, and different through excessive discernment and assimilation).

Liberace, with his glorious display of attire and millions of devoted maternal fans, had his Venus in Cancer quindecile his Moon in Sagittarius (the emotional need to share personal philosophies and beliefs met through the use of aesthetics and kinship).

Ansel Adams, photographer of black-and-white photographs whose work is known for its stark contrasts, has his Mars in Pisces quindecile his Moon in Leo (the emotional need to creatively express oneself met through application of sensitivity and working with the intangible).

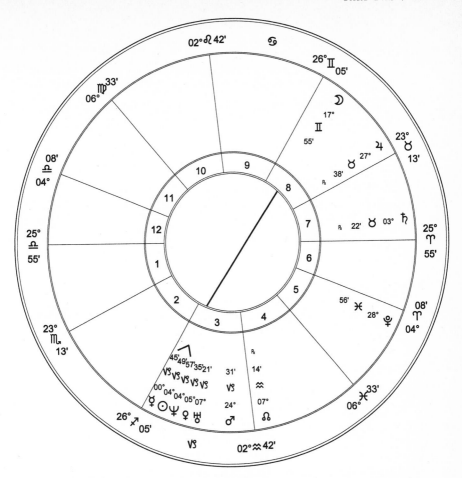

Horoscope 6
Louis Pasteur / December 27, 1822 / Dole, France / 2:00 A.M. LMT

Louis Pasteur developed the "germ theory of disease," one of the most important contributions in the history of medicine. His work became the foundation of microbiology, which is the cornerstone of modern medicine. His work in understanding the transmission of and immunization against disease is unsurpassed in its impact upon the health and welfare of the people of our times. The use of sterilization of surgical instruments and medical supplies began because of his discoveries on the control of infectious disease. He went on to discover the three basic bacteria that are responsible for all human illnesses, and his development of the process of "pasteurization," through which harmful microbes in perishable foods are destroyed by heat without destroying the food itself, was revolutionary.

Pasteur's life was devoted to research and the improvement of scientific understanding. He was a man who never put forth a premise or a theory unless, as he put it, "it could be proven by experimentation." Fully aware of the international importance of his work, he ascribed particular importance to the spread of knowledge and application of research worldwide.

Louis Pasteur had three planets quindecile his Moon. His Mercury in Capricorn (use of intelligence, mental comprehension, and communication through hard work, ambition, and tangible goals) was quindecile his Moon in Gemini (the emotional need to be informed). The need for physical proof to substantiate the correctness of his theories was, by his own admission, a constant focus.

Likewise, his Sun in Capricorn (recognition sought through hard work, ambition, and tangible goals) was quindecile his Moon in Gemini. This push for ego recognition for the use of his mind and ideas was a strong influence on the manifestation of his life.

Pasteur also had his Neptune in Capricorn (a seeking of the illusive, imaginary, and ideal within ambitions and goals) quindecile his Moon in Gemini. This quindecile provided him with the ambition and drive needed to prove that the unknown can be as substantive as the physical reality we know to be true.

Any one of these quindeciles could and would account for his interest in science and research, but the combination of all three literally thrust him into a life of continual seeking of scientific knowledge for the benefit of us all.

The Sun and Moon

The Sun quindecile the Moon is one of the rarest and most difficult aspects to understand. The intensity of this combination can enmesh the personality into a singular focus of doing whatever is necessary to get one's security needs met through ego recognition. Emotional security needs, or perhaps insecurity, drive the individual to gain ego recognition from the outside world. There can be an almost narcissistic quality to this particular combination that, if left unchecked, can create great difficulty. The focus on recognition can become so intense that the individual will do almost anything to get the attention that he or she craves. This combination is about developing a relationship with one's self. However, until the individual begins to understand how to accomplish this, he or she may be driven by a need to attain recognition and approval from others. These relationships can be one-on-one relationships, or they can be focused toward seeking recognition from the world at large through the development of some kind of public persona.

> *Sarah Ferguson,* wife of Prince Andrew who found herself constantly on center stage and couldn't quite "get it right" until after her divorce and semiwithdrawal from the glaring limelight, has her Sun in Libra quindecile her Moon in Aries (recognition sought through relationship to meet personal and self-focused emotional needs).

> *Joseph Mengele,* known as the "Angel of Death" for his cruel and painful pseudoscientific experiments on inmates in the Nazi concentration camps, had no qualms about the pain and suffering he caused. His Sun in Pisces was quindecile his Moon in Libra (recognition sought through working with the intangible to meet the emotional need of being appreciated).

> *B. F. Skinner,* noted psychologist who upset the entire psychological community with his controlled scientific methods of research on behavior being linked to a person's response to his or her environment, had his Sun in Aries quindecile his Moon in Virgo (recognition sought through self-focused means to meet the emotional needs of discernment and assimilation).

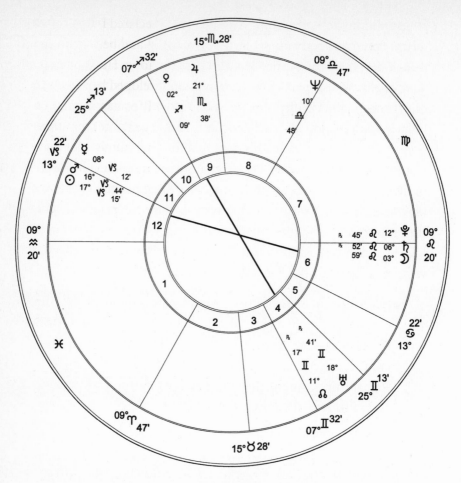

Horoscope 7
David Bowie / January 8, 1947 / Brixton, England / 9:15 A.M. GMT

David Bowie has produced and presented some of the most outrageous shows ever done through his exotic image, all flash and glitter, combined with weird sensational effects. He is perhaps one of the most internationally well-known rock stars of our time.

He was born illegitimate to middle-class parents in a midsize town in England. He had a half-brother, whom he idolized, who was nine years his elder and who was diagnosed paranoid schizophrenic and eventually committed suicide by throwing himself under a train.

According to Bowie, at the age of eight he declared his intention to become "the greatest rock star in England,"[1] and began his musical career that year with the gift of a saxophone. He formed his first rock band at the age of seventeen and developed his androgynous persona by the age of nineteen. He openly touted his bisexuality in both his public and private life, which generated headline-grabbing press stories. His music became the banner of a new generation, and he was acclaimed on both sides of the Atlantic. He went on to work in films, as well as continuing his musical career, and today at the age of fifty-two he is still a force in the world of rock and roll.

Bowie has his Sun in Capricorn (recognition sought through hard work, ambition, and tangible goals) quindecile his Moon in Leo (the emotional need to express the self creatively). This is the obsessive-compulsive thrust that drove him to become the superstar personality that he was and still is today.

Compounding this is his Mars in Capricorn (energy and action applied to hard work, ambition, and tangible goals) quindecile his Moon in Leo. Here is the physical strength, stamina, and great panache expressed in his performances.

In addition, Bowie has his Uranus in Gemini (disruption of the status quo through communication of ideas and information) quindecile his Venus in Sagittarius (aesthetics and kinship within philosophies and beliefs). Is it any wonder that we have all heard and read about his flamboyant lifestyle and sexual exploits?

Personal Planet Quindecile Personal Planet

When a personal planet is quindecile a second personal planet (i.e., the Sun, Moon, Mercury, Venus, and Mars), the manifestation of the aspect will be shown in the personality through the nature and dynamics of the two planets involved. For instance, if Mars is quindecile Mercury, there will be a need to take action on ideas and information, or if Mars is quindecile Venus, there will be a need to take action on aesthetics and kinship.

For your reference, the most basic nature of the personal planets can be expressed as follows: the Sun seeks recognition, the Moon seeks security, Mercury seeks information, Venus seeks kinship, and Mars seeks action.

Jack Nicholson, legendary film star who has played numerous unforgettable movie roles and is known for pursuing anything and everything that grabs his attention, has his Mars in Sagittarius quindecile his Mercury in Taurus (action within philosophies and belief systems through physical understanding).

Freddie Prinze, well-known comedian of the 1980s who entertained us through his wit and sharp repartee, had his Mars in Capricorn quindecile his Mercury in Cancer (action applied within ambitions through communication with the family and the people).

H. R. Halderman, White House chief of staff during the Watergate scandal who was deeply involved in the cover-up because of his close relationship with President Richard M. Nixon, had his Mars in Taurus quindecile his Venus in Libra (tangible action applied within kinship and collaboration through all to which it relates).

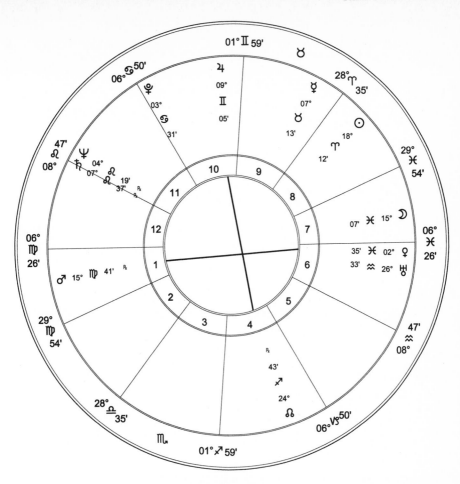

Horoscope 8
Betty Ford / April 8, 1918 / Chicago, IL / 3:45 P.M. CST

Betty Ford, wife of the thirty-eighth president of the United States, will probably always be remembered for two very different issues, both of which affected her personally. Because of her position as first lady, almost anything of note in her life rocketed through the media and became public domain for us all to examine. We can be proud and grateful that she allowed us to view those parts of her life that were most difficult.

Prior to her marriage, Ford was a professional dancer, fashion coordinator, and model. She has always put a great deal of energy and focus into her life, but quite naturally becoming the wife of a politician dictated much of how the world would see and remember her. What she always showed to us on the outside was the epitome of the polite and proper political wife who knew how to handle all the demands of that position appropriately.

In reality, Betty Ford was an alcoholic who drank secretly to deal with the intensity of a life that was not her own. She took this part of her life, which was societally shameful and misunderstood at that time, and brought it into public view. She focused not only on her personal recovery, but used this as a springboard to establish the Betty Ford Center for the treatment of addictions.

She also developed breast cancer, which resulted in a mastectomy. The courage she exhibited in sharing her own experience with us brought this issue "out of the closet," again, at a time in our society when we were reluctant to deal publicly with anything that intimate and personal, despite the fact that many women were dealing with it privately. She was instrumental in a dramatic increase in early diagnosis and prevention of this terrible disease.

Betty Ford has her Mars in Virgo (application of discernment and assimilation) quindecile her Venus in Pisces (sensitivity and working with the intangible through kinship and cooperation). The dynamics of this configuration can not only be seen through the early professional focus, but also throughout her life as a whole. Certainly this aspect would have been a major factor in the development of her alcoholism, taking into account the illusive qualities of addiction; however, it would likewise have been a major influence in her providing us with a magnificent demonstration of how one can redirect a problematic predisposition and turn it into a positive benefit.

She also has her Jupiter in Gemini (excess, expansion, and growth through information and ideas) quindecile her North Node in Sagittarius (the life purpose through philosophies and belief systems). The strength of her public profile, and the sharing of herself and her life with us, has, in my opinion, fulfilled that function.

Societal or Generational Planet
Quindecile Personal Planet

The zodiacal position of the societal planets (i.e., Jupiter and Saturn) are an indicator of the trends and fashions of the times, and the generational planets (i.e., Uranus, Neptune, and Pluto) are indicators of the movements of consciousness. If we consider Jupiter to be the "great optimist and expander," Saturn the "realist and boundary setter," Uranus the "revolutionary," Neptune the "unifier," and Pluto the "transformer," it is interesting to watch how these planets tend to influence our society as a whole. If we look at the ebb and flow of social trends and generational issues, there is almost always a big push to promote (Jupiter) whatever the trend may be at the time, followed by a societal reaction of "No! This isn't going to happen," or "enough is enough" (Saturn), then a cultural revolution (Uranus) to express personal freedoms, followed by a unifying process (Neptune), and ending with a societal transformation or shift as a whole (Pluto).

Therefore, when a societal or generational planet is in quindecile aspect to a personal planet, there is an underlying potential to either be a leader in setting the current crazes and fads of the time or to perhaps "get caught up" in them. Depending on the nature of the personal planet that is being aspected, this quindecile can be demonstrated through how the individual communicates and acts, or in the friends and social circles toward which he or she gravitates.

> *Carry Nation* was a leader of the Temperance Movement in the 1860s who preached the "evils of drink" and stormed into saloons and smashed up supplies of beer and spirits. She had her Jupiter in Gemini quindecile her Venus in Scorpio (excessive ideas focused within collaborative efforts for control and transformation).

> *James Dean,* the original "rebel without a cause" who introduced an entire generation of young adolescents and teenagers to the

idea of becoming their own authority in life, had his Saturn in Capricorn quindecile his Mars in Leo (demonstration of authority through applied action within creative self-expression).

Karl Marx, social theorist and philosopher who developed the economic concept of socialism, had his Uranus in Sagittarius quindecile his Mercury in Gemini (disruption of belief systems through communication of new and innovative ideas).

Joan of Arc, who through her spiritual visions at the age of seventeen inspired the ruler of France to give her an army to fight the English, had her Neptune in Cancer quindecile her Venus in Capricorn (seeking the ideal for all the people through kinship and collaboration within a leadership role).

Paramahansa Yogananda, founder of the Self-Realization Movement, which utilizes scientific methods of meditation and principles of spiritual living, had his Pluto in Gemini quindecile his Mercury in Sagittarius (powerful perspectives communicated through belief systems).

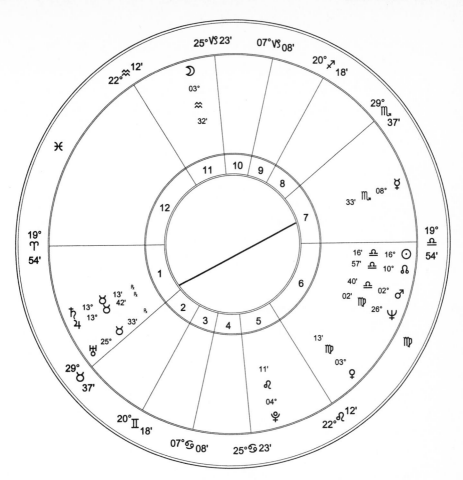

Horoscope 9
John Lennon / October 9, 1940 / Liverpool, England / 6:30 P.M. GMD

John Lennon was a songwriter, musician, and megastar of the 1960s and 1970s, as a member of the Beatles. He not only had a major impact on the music industry, but also on an entire generation of youth by leading a counterculture into its own power.

John was reportedly born in the middle of an air raid during World War II. His parents separated when he was four years old, and he went to live with his Aunt Mimi. His father was a merchant seaman and John saw little of him. His early life was not terrible, but it was not great either. John lived in the chaos of drug addiction for most of his adult life and died at the hands of an assassin at the age of forty.

The Beatles, as a group, literally rocked the world with their "new sound," and the "hippie generation" was born. Psychedelic music became all the rage as the youth of that time went into major rebellion against home, authority, and whatever else happened to interfere with their good times.

John, however, was more than just his music. He carried the banner against the Vietnam War and not only coined the phrase "make love not war," but became the living model of that philosophy. His music was the theme of the times, culminating in 1972 with his writing and recording of the song "Give Peace a Chance."

John Lennon had his Uranus in Taurus (disruption of the status quo with innovative ideas through tangible means) quindecile his Mercury in Scorpio (communication of transformative ideas). His ideas and his music were groundbreaking. There may still be some dispute about how much practicality he used in his methods for getting his point across, but his success in doing so cannot be disputed. He carried a message that ultimately was a significant force in ending the Vietnam War.

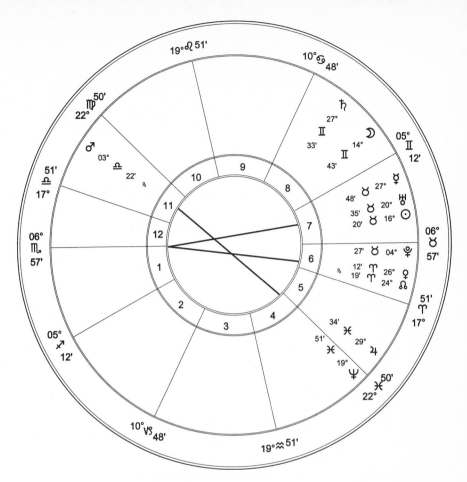

Horoscope 10
Sigmund Freud / May 6, 1856 / Freiberg, Germany / 6:30 P.M. LMT

Sigmund Freud, known as the "Father of Psychoanalysis," devoted his life to the exploration, understanding, and healing of the human psyche. His work focused on looking at the power of the subconscious mind. Although his theories were first disputed, his work became the foundation for treating psychiatric disorders through psychoanalysis.

Freud's early interest in science and human personality led him to obtain a degree at the age of twenty-five from the University of Vienna Medical School, specializing in neurology. This training in

neurology left him with an ambition to find the connections between the biological and psychological interplay of the mind. Although he was initially dedicated to research, financial considera-
tions led him to become a clinician. His patients became the
primary source for his research and writings.

Freud's interest in dreams, as a signifier of underlying unresolved
psychological factors, began with an interpretation of one of his own
dreams in 1885 and set off his lifelong journey to understand the
subconscious mind. This journey took him to Paris that same year,
where he focused on hysteria, hypnosis, and the power of suggestion,
in collaboration with Jean-Martin Charcot with whom he coau-
thored the groundbreaking work *Studies in Hysteria*. Working with
others, while initially successful, only lasted for limited periods of
time. Freud's push to put his theories forward created difficulty in
maintaining collaborative relationships.

One of Freud's greatest contributions to the psychological com-
munity was the authoring of *The Interpretation of Dreams*, which
was published in 1889. In that work, he noted that "dreams are a
wish fulfillment" and that "fantasy provides clues to the subconscious," relating that internal censors edit our dreams and transform
the dream content into disguised desires in an acceptable form.

Sigmund Freud holds a firm lead in the hierarchy of psychological masters through his work on free association, the Oedipus and
Electra complexes, the understanding of the Ego, Super Ego, and Id,
the dynamics of repression, and the relevance of unconscious sexual
urges. These works changed our understanding of the human psyche forever.

Freud's horoscope contains two quindeciles that involve generational planets. His Uranus in Taurus (disruption of the status quo
through the use of innovative ideas) was quindecile his Ascendant
(the outer personality) in Scorpio (through transformation, regeneration, or control). This was his obsession and compulsion with
putting his work out for all to receive.

Additionally, his Neptune in Pisces (seeking the illusive, imaginary, and ideal through sensitivity, intuitiveness, and working with the intangible) was quindecile his Mars in Libra (application of energy and action through all to which it relates). This describes his drive to understand the human psyche from which we have all benefited so much.

Freud's North Node in Aries (the life purpose through personal and self-focused means) was quindecile his Scorpio Ascendant (transformation or controlled outer personality). He followed his life purpose through his devotion to his transformative psychological work.

To quote Freud, "In my youth I felt an overpowering need to understand something of the riddles of the world in which we live and perhaps even to contribute something to their solution."[2] This one simple comment shows the indisputable power of the quindeciles in his horoscope.

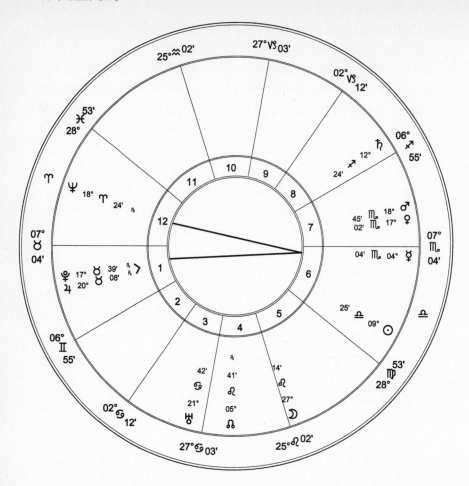

Horoscope 11
Mohandas Gandhi / October 2, 1869 / Porbandar, India /
7:11 P.M. LMT

Mohandas Gandhi was the leader of the nonviolent freedom movement that eventually led to the independence of India. He possessed
an inner strength and determination that was unsurpassed, leading
his people out of tyranny and bondage.

Gandhi was educated in Great Britain and attained a law degree. Upon his return to India, he found that not only had his
mother passed away, but that his prospects of a prominent legal
career were very slim. He then moved to South Africa, where he

began to become known for standing up for his political beliefs, despite retribution.

Upon his return to India, he rapidly became a primary force in both the promotion and advancement of civil rights and in the politics of India. He became India's most powerful and influential spiritual and political leader. His message of nonviolent protest, in the form of boycotts of British goods and services, led to his arrest on numerous occasions. He demonstrated personal sacrifice to his people and the entire world through periods of fasting to near-death. Gandhi lived in communal, below-poverty-level circumstances, and continued peaceful protest despite humiliation and force used against him by the British. This made him a spiritual and political champion who could not be denied. Indian freedom and unity were his focus. Despite all the difficulties he faced, he carried that message until the day he was shot to death on his way to evening prayer.

His spiritual beliefs centered around several simple concepts. He believed all men are brothers; therefore he would not raise up his hand against anyone despite what they might do. In his words, he believed "in the absoluteness of God, and, therefore in humanity," and that "in seeking to know the truth we seek to know God."[3] Through the demonstration of his own life, we see his belief that if we simplify our lives and give up our worldly possessions, we set our souls free.

Gandhi had his Mercury (use of intelligence and communication) quindecile one societal planet and two generational planets. The enormous impact of these aspects coming together in one horoscope, combined with other astrological configurations, propelled him into the position of effective spokesperson for such a major undertaking.

Gandhi had his Jupiter in Taurus (excess, expansion, and growth through a practical and tangible approach) quindecile his Mercury in Scorpio (communication of transformative ideas). His passionate belief that India must become self-sufficient in order to be free was not only heard but seen through his continuous weaving of home-spun cloth and working in his own vegetable garden.

Likewise, his Pluto in Taurus (empowerment or disempowerment through a practical and tangible approach) was quindecile his Mercury in Scorpio. It was his ability to communicate his perspectives, not only through written and verbal means but also through how he lived his own life, that made Gandhi such a powerful model of humanitarianism.

Compounding this was his Neptune in Aries (seeking the illusive, imaginary, and ideal through personal and self-focused means) quindecile his Mercury in Scorpio. It surely must have been his obsession with, as he put it, "the absoluteness of God" that gave Gandhi the inner strength to endure all that he did and to still look at his fellow human beings with unconditional love and acceptance.

Outer Planet Quindecile Outer Planet

The alignment of outer planets to other outer planets is suggestive of how we define the times in which we live. These alignments reflect the movements, events, and issues on a societal, national, and global level that impact our consciousness and lives as a whole. In understanding the slow movement of the outer planets in our solar system, we are conscious of the fact that millions and perhaps even billions of people are born during the time span of these alignments. They are therefore considered to be "signs of the times," rather than significant indicators of an individual's personal response or approach toward life.

This is not to say, however, that individuals born in times of outer planetary alignments may not be involved in the issues of those times. When this is the case, there will be additional configurations in their horoscopes that reflect the dynamics of their active participation on a personal level.

There is an opportunity for each planet to make a quindecile twice during its cycle (in relation to a second planet), with one alignment being on each side of the opposition point of that second planet. The first quindecile will be made during the planet's approach toward the opposition point of the second planet, and the next quindecile will be made during the planet's separation from the opposition point of the second planet. Taking into account the normal cycle of each of the planets in our solar system, and given our knowledge of the individual speeds of those planets, we are gifted with the knowledge that there is a regular and predictable pattern to the time spans between aspectual alignments.

The time span between the first and second quindecile alignment will be of relatively short length, because of the short distance between those two points. In fact, there is only approximately a 30° span (or distance) between the approaching and separating alignments. The next time span, which would be between a separating and an approaching alignment, is immensely longer because the distance between these two points is approximately a 330° span (or distance).

If we look back historically over the last 1,000 years at the times when the outer planets (Uranus, Neptune, and Pluto) have come into quindecile alignment, it is very interesting to see the patterns contained in those alignments.

Uranus Quindecile Neptune

Uranus quindecile Neptune happens approximately every 150 to 160 years, with the secondary quindecile again in another fifteen to twenty years. It appears to reference time periods of disruption of the status quo (Uranus) within a seeking of the ideal (Neptune), or perhaps the awakening (Uranus) of a vision (Neptune).

1043–1058—There was upheaval in the Roman church that resulted in the permanent separation between Rome and the Eastern church.

1215–1230—The Magna Carta, which gave rights to common people for the first time, was signed and implemented.

1389–1402—The Turkish invasions were finally turned around, which ultimately led to a Christian Europe. (At this same time, Uranus was quindecile Pluto.)

1556–1573—Queen Elizabeth took the throne, and the extension of the British Empire began.

1727–1743—The Age of Enlightenment began, which resulted in philosophical, religious, and political ideology and expansion into the New World.

1898–1918—This was a time of wars, including the war between Spain and the United States, the Boxer Rebellion in China, the Boer War, and the beginning of World War I.

2070–2090—

Uranus Quindecile Pluto

Uranus quindecile Pluto happens approximately every 100 to 130 years, with the secondary quindecile in another eight to eleven years. This appears to reference time periods of disruption of the status quo (Uranus) within a shift in the perspectives of consciousness (Pluto), or perhaps a shifting (Uranus) of power (Pluto), or even an awakening (Uranus) to transformation (Pluto).

1022–1033—This was the beginning of individuated thought that eventually resulted in the upheaval of the Roman church.

1138–1147—The Second Crusade.

1278–1290—The beginning of innovative thought and technological discovery.

1392–1400—This was the beginning of the Renaissance, which was a time of revolution in science, art, and philosophy.

1533–1544—Henry VIII fought Rome and founded the Church of England.

1645–1653—The English Civil War and upheaval with Scotland.

1790–1799—The Industrial Revolution was in full swing. The French Revolution had begun, leading to the rise of Napoleon and ultimately the establishment of the French Republic.

1898–1906—The beginning of our modern world through the invention of the telegraph, the end of steam and the beginning of the electrical age, and the birth of the theory of relativity. Psychoanalysis was born, and travel expanded with the flight of the Wright brothers, the automobile, and the assembly line.

2044–2053—

Neptune Quindecile Pluto

Neptune quindecile Pluto happens approximately every 500 years, with the secondary quindecile in another twenty-six to twenty-seven years. With only two time periods to explore, it is difficult to define the impact of these alignments into one central theme.

1139–1166—A time of forceful spiritual pursuit incorporating the Second Crusade, the first use of explosives by the Chinese, and the birth of Genghis Khan.

1633–1660—A time of spiritual development with the founding of new churches, including the Baptist Church, the Quaker Movement, and the end of torture in England.

2126–2153—

Planet Quindecile the North Node

Not being an expert on the South Node, I will only work with planets quindecile the North Node in this book. When interpreting any horoscope, it is important to understand the different levels of information that the nodal axis may suggest. My research has shown that there are three distinctly different possibilities of manifestation. Quindeciles to the nodal axis may suggest the soul's evolutionary development through following the life purpose, a thrust into public recognition and renown, or a prominent maternal relationship influencing one's life.

Expression of the Quindecile
Through the Traditional Role of the North Node

The first avenue of expression is through the traditional role of the North Node. Historically, this role has been to signify the areas of development in this particular lifetime in the evolutionary journey of the soul. Manifesting the potential of one's North Node is thought to be particularly difficult, because the areas involved are only in the beginning stages of development. A quindecile to this sensitive point intensifies the need for the individual to work toward the integration of that area of life into his or her soul's growth, and it actually becomes the individual's "life purpose."

> *Margaret Thatcher,* the first female prime minister of Great Britain, has her Jupiter in Capricorn quindecile her North Node in Leo (following the life purpose within expression of philosophies and opinions by hard work, ambition, and tangible goals through strong development of ego).

> *John F. Kennedy,* past president of the United States who became involved in politics as a result of his brother's death rather than by his own desire, had his Saturn in Cancer quindecile his North Node in Capricorn (following the life path through responsibility to the family and the people by hard work, ambition, and tangible goals).

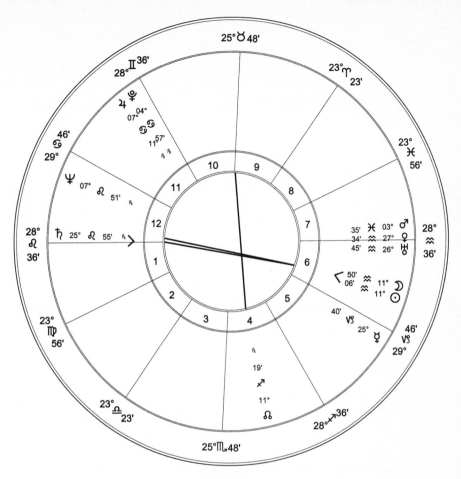

Horoscope 12
Jackie Robinson / January 31, 1919 / Cairo, GA / 6:30 P.M. CST

Jackie Robinson, despite his undeniable talent as a professional baseball player, is perhaps remembered more for breaking the color barrier in major league baseball than for his actual playing of the game.

Born into an impoverished Southern black family, he was the youngest of five children. His father, who was a sharecropper, left the family, and his mother worked as a domestic. Jackie excelled in all sports and earned varsity letters at UCLA in football, basketball, baseball, and track. He served in the U.S. Army during World War

II and took the baseball field for the first time in April 1947 at the age of twenty-eight.

He left his natural combativeness in the locker room and took his talents and determination onto the field. He endured incredible abuse without fighting back. He let his batting and base running speak for him. His powerful presence in the sport of baseball and his skilled use of his God-given talents culminated in his being elected to the Baseball Hall of Fame in 1962.

In 1963, after he retired from baseball, he began to speak out about racial injustice. He traveled to Birmingham, Alabama, to be with Martin Luther King, Jr., and was in the forefront of the demonstrations at that time. He became a forceful civil rights advocate and fought for this cause until his death.

Jackie Robinson had his North Node in Sagittarius (the life purpose focused through philosophies and belief systems) quindecile his Taurus Midheaven (career focus and societal position through practical and tangible means). The thrust of his belief that all people are created equal was seen throughout his entire life, through all that he accomplished and the public profile taken through his choice of career. The popularity he enjoyed in his career provided him with the opportunity to voice his beliefs and have them heard by others.

Jackie also had his Ascendant and Saturn in Leo (the outer personality creatively expresses responsibility and authority) quindecile his Sun and Moon in Aquarius (the emotional need for recognition of doing something significant, unusual, and different). This was the reserve and focused strength of character that was needed for him to make a difference in this world, in a way that society could not and would not deny. His life purpose was indeed fulfilled. It was a mandate of Jackie's life that he be seen and known for making a significant contribution to the world.

Expression of the Quindecile
Through Recognition and Renown

The second avenue of expression of a planet quindecile the North Node is a strong push toward recognition and renown. The focus of the quindecile is literally "thrust" upon the individual and comes almost as a byproduct of the manifestation of his or her life. It is not that these individuals necessarily focus on a need to be in the limelight, but life circumstances tend to push fame and public attention upon them, whether they are looking for it or not. It can be suggestive of a life that is somehow destined to be in the limelight.

Jeffrey Dahmer, the serial killer, not only had bizarre homosexual relations with at least twelve young men, but also murdered them and dismembered their bodies. He was able to elude capture for years despite keeping various body parts in his apartment without detection. Dahmer had his Mars in Aries quindecile his North Node in Virgo (recognition and renown through assimilation of energy and action within personal and self-focused means).

O. J. Simpson, already a famous football player and well-known in the United States, became infamous worldwide when he was accused of the savage murder of his wife, Nicole Brown Simpson, and her friend Ron Goldman. Despite this he still lives with a certain panache and remains, to many, an unjustly accused hero. Simpson has his Jupiter in Scorpio quindecile his North Node in Leo (excessive control driven by ego brings recognition and renown).

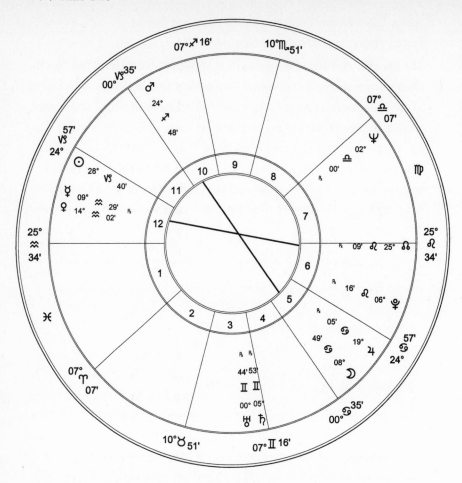

Horoscope 13
Janis Joplin / January 19, 1943 / Port Arthur, TX / 9:45 A.M. CST

Janis Joplin, known as the "Judy Garland of rock," became the female symbol of "sex, drugs, and rock-and-roll" for the "Hippie Generation" of the 1960s. Her music and her rasping, gut-wrenching, plaintive wail not only stirred the senses of that generation, but still today, thirty years later, are acclaimed by millions, and her music remains popular with each new generation of youth.

Janis was born into a middle-class family in a small, Gulf Coast refinery town in Texas, as one of three children. There was nothing special about her life or her childhood that would point to a potential to rocket into superstardom, although it has been said that she always felt different and somehow set apart from her friends and classmates. She was raised in a very segregated Southern town, and could never understand why there should have to be a difference in the treatment of blacks and whites.

As a teenager, she was extremely bright, but also overweight, with a face full of pimples. She suffered numerous rejections in high school from those who did not understand her, and while attending the University of Texas in 1963, she was voted "The Ugliest Man on Campus." This led to her leaving Texas and hitchhiking to San Francisco in search of a new life and a venue for her music. Her adolescence was a painful memory for the rest of her short adult life. Perhaps it was her own personal torment, at the teenage rejections she suffered, that led her to a love of the "blues."

As her stardom increased, so did Janis' addictions. She was a workaholic, and her use of alcohol and drugs is almost as legendary as her brash-speaking, flamboyant public persona. At the age of twenty-seven, Janis died alone in a Los Angeles hotel room from an overdose of heroin. She is gone but will never be forgotten, for her music lives on in the hearts of her fans.

Janis Joplin had her Mercury in Aquarius (communication of the significant, unusual, and different) quindecile her North Node in Leo (recognition and renown through creative self-expression). Her unique style of music not only conveyed a message to which everyone could relate, it also created a great deal of controversy because of its nonmelodic and sometimes ear-splitting sound.

Supplementing this was her Mars in Sagittarius (action within philosophies and beliefs) quindecile her Moon in Cancer (the need for emotional connection through the family and people). The sharing of her excessive lifestyle, her belief in societal equality for all, and the projection of her pain were Janis' means of emotionally connecting to the world.

Expression of the Quindecile
Through the Maternal Relationship

The last avenue of expression for a planet quindecile the North Node is seen through the maternal relationship. The impact of the individual's relationship with the mother is a primary factor in the molding of the individual's character, demeanor, values, and ability to cope or not cope with the life manifestation. The strength or lack of strength of this relationship can be clearly seen through either its positive or negative projection.

> *Woody Allen,* the diminutive neurotic who has written, directed, and acted in numerous films centering around psychological dysfunction and emotional self-doubt, has his Pluto in Cancer (empowerment or disempowerment through the family) quindecile his North Node in Capricorn (the maternal influence focused through the career and societal position). Woody had a love-hate relationship with his mother. She was physically abusive to him as a child, yet supported his career in his adult life. Woody has stated that her "Groucho Marx sense of humor" was instrumental in the development of his own comedic style.[4]

> *Prince William of England,* who is known to have been very close to his mother, Princess Diana, until her death in 1997, has his North Node in Cancer (the maternal relationship through the family and the people) quindecile his Sagittarius Ascendant (philosophies and belief systems shown through the outer personality). I believe that, as heir to the throne of England, Prince William may be the one to finally bring a warm and human face to this historically stoic and unemotional family. The imprint of his mother's love for the people and her spontaneous warmth with the public will surely impact how his personality is projected as Great Britain's future king.

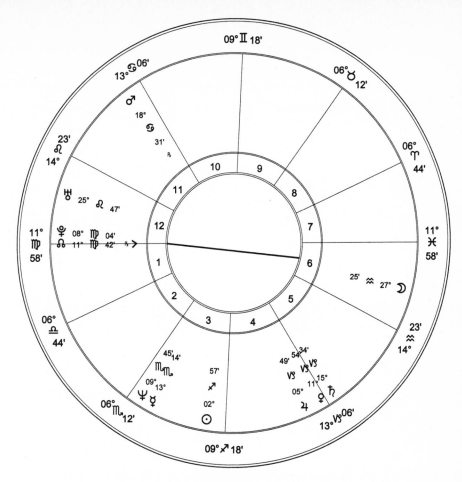

Horoscope 14
John F. Kennedy, Jr. / November 25, 1960 / Washington, D.C. /
12:22 A.M. EST

John F. Kennedy, Jr., was the son of American president John F. Kennedy, Sr., and Jacqueline Kennedy Onassis. He has been a part of our "American family" since the assassination of his father in 1963. The image of a small boy saluting his father's coffin as it rolled by, on a cold November morning, is etched into the hearts of Americans forever.

After the death of his father, John Jr. was raised primarily by his mother, Jackie Kennedy. Despite the fact that she remarried,

Jackie let it be known that John and his sister were her children and that the responsibility for ensuring their emotional well-being lay with her. To say that Jackie rose to that calling would be an understatement.

It is well-known that John's mother was the primary influence in his life, and not only did he have a close personal relationship with her, he followed her advice and counsel closely. By his own admission, he learned his values and his awareness of political issues from her. She taught him the need to set a good example not only through the manner in which he lived his own life, but also through his treatment of others. He even followed her into the publishing field, although her focus was books and his was a political magazine. According to relatives and close family friends, it was Jackie's love of the written word that was instrumental in the development of John's literary interests and his decision to found his magazine, *George*.

John had his Moon in Aquarius (the emotional need to do something significant, unusual, and different) quindecile his North Node in Virgo (the maternal influence through discernment and assimilation). The influence of his mother was indisputable, especially in encouraging him to think for himself and to hold true to his own ideas.

John also had his Moon quindecile his Virgo Ascendant (the outer personality). It is difficult for anyone who is born in the spotlight to live a "normal" life, especially when the media is recording your every step and breath, but somehow John did just that. The image he showed to all of us was one of not only a "normal" young man, but also a caring and sincere person.

John's recent accidental death was a shock to all of us, and we are left wondering what impact he would have made with the rest of his life had he lived longer. I believe that he did something significant, unusual, and different by showing us all that it is possible to become a positive influence in the world despite early life trauma, constant media coverage, and the pressure of always having to somehow live up to a nation's expectations.

1. See George Tremlett, *David Bowie: Living on the Brink* (New York, NY: Carroll & Graf, 1996) 12.

2. See the Library of Congress Exhibitions Internet website, "Freud: Section One: Formative Years," http://lcweb.loc.gov/exhibits/freud/freud01.html.

3. See Leigh Angela's Internet website *Gandhi: Living in Peace*, http://gandhi.virtualave.net/.

4. See Lee Guthrie, *Woody Allen: A Biography* (New York, NY: Drake Publishers, 1978) 9.

PART III

Astrological Analysis of the Quindecile

The Jupiter Factor

Since Jupiter (the largest planet in our solar system) symbolizes excess, expansion, growth, overabundance, enlargement, indulgence, and so on, it should not be surprising to see it engaged during time periods of heightened obsessive-compulsive behavior. After all, Jupiter's function within astrological configurations is to broaden and promote development in the areas of life that it is directed toward in the horoscope.

In the course of my research, I have repeatedly found Jupiter to be involved during times of extreme obsessive-compulsive focus. This involvement, whether it be through Jupiter's natal placement or through Jupiter activating a natal quindecile by means of progression or transit, happens approximately 68 percent of the time. Jupiter's influence, and its affinity with the dynamics of the quindecile, can arouse an otherwise relatively dormant configuration and stimulate increased manifestation of obsessive-compulsive behaviors into the forefront of an individual's life.

Retrograde Planets

At this point, it is important to discuss the dynamics involved when one, or sometimes both, of the planets in the quindecile aspect are retrograde. This is certainly not an unusual occurrence. As a matter of fact, more often than not, the slower-moving planet will be retrograde because of the dynamics of that particular astrological phenomena.

In the extensive research I have done, I have come to the conclusion that there is no special significance to a planet being retrograde while in quindecile alignment. A retrograde planet is a retrograde planet, and the fact that a planet is retrograding within this particular aspect is no different than if it were to be retrograding within an opposition, inconjunct, or square aspect. The same dynamics of interpretation regarding that particular planet will hold true no matter what aspectual alignment is present.

CHAPTER 6

Dynamics of Natal Interpretation

It is important to emphasize once again that the presence of a particular aspect, or planetary combination, is not the sole influence that determines personality development and the manner in which an individual lives his or her life. The natal horoscope can only suggest and reference the basic makeup of the individual. It provides us with possibilities and probabilities of predisposed vulnerability to stimulators and stressors that may be present in the early environment. It is each individual's personal reactions and responses to these developmental dynamics that ultimately determine how any particular planetary combination may actually manifest in that individual's life.

Therefore, we must synthesize the horoscope as a whole and not just look at one configuration contained in that horoscope. We must understand the implications of each planetary placement by house, sign, and aspect, and then bring all that information together in order to get a complete picture of the individual.

When interpreting the natal horoscope, we can find many different suggestions and possibilities. The objective, when synthesizing the interaction of the planetary positions, is to find a main focus or repetitive theme in the horoscope. It is well accepted, throughout the astrological world, that if a particular issue or suggestion is a major part of the "life blueprint," it will be referenced in the horoscope through several different configurations.

A wonderful example of different styles of manifestation for the same astrological configuration can be seen in the lives of Walt Disney and Jimmy Hoffa. They both had Neptune in Cancer (seeking the illusive, imaginary, and ideal through the family and the people) quindecile Jupiter in Capricorn (excess, expansion, and growth through hard work, ambition, and tangible goals). Walt Disney utilized this quindecile to create Mickey Mouse and Disneyland, while Jimmy Hoffa focused it in the development of the Brotherhood of Teamsters and its alliances with the Mafia.

While it is not my intention in this book to provide a complete horoscope analysis of individual examples used, I do believe that it will be helpful for the reader to become aware of how other supporting planetary alignments impact the adverse or successful manifestation of the quindecile aspect.

If we will look back at some of the personalities we have already explored and examine their complete horoscopes, and not only their quindecile configurations, we will see that there are additional planetary placements supporting the direction or emphasis of the quindecile manifestation. We will also do this with an example of a horoscope that we have not yet discussed to see how it all fits together from the beginning of the analysis to completion.

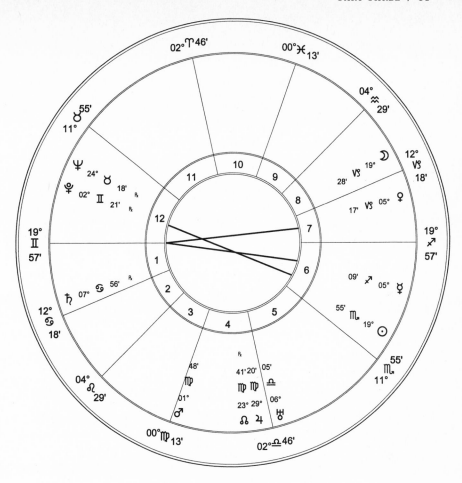

Horoscope 15
General George S. Patton, Jr. / November 11, 1885 / San Marino, CA /
6:36 P.M. PST / (supporting alignments)

General George S. Patton, Jr., had his Pluto in Gemini (empowerment or disempowerment through ideas and information) opposed his Mercury in Sagittarius (communication of philosophies
and belief systems). Both these planetary placements squared his
Mars in Scorpio (application of control). Pluto resided in his
twelfth house (karma, self-undoing, unconscious impulses, and
spiritual connection). This certainly didn't bode well for him, unless his focus was through development and use of the spiritual

possibilities contained in that house. Pluto ruled his sixth house (service, health, the workplace, and relationships with coworkers). Therefore the tension contained in the dynamics of Pluto's placement would be played out in those areas. Mercury resided in his sixth house and ruled his fourth house (home, emotional security, and early nurturing). His fourth house contained Mars, which is part of this difficult configuration. This is suggestive of early life home difficulties having a strong impact on how he communicated his perspectives and the actions he took, all of which would flow into his daily work and his relationships within his work.

His Sun in Scorpio (recognition sought through control) and Mercury in Sagittarius also resided in his sixth house. His Sun opposed his Neptune in Taurus (seeking the illusive, imaginary, and ideal through tangible means). Additionally, Neptune resided in his twelfth house and also ruled his Midheaven (external focus through career and societal position). This was, again, a warning flag of potential difficulty, because of Patton's intense need for recognition of his ideas and beliefs and the probability that he would not get the control he sought in his career.

Patton also had his Venus in Capricorn (aesthetics and kinship within hard work, ambition, and tangible goals) opposed his Saturn in Cancer (responsibility and authority through the family and the people). Saturn resided in his first house (self) and ruled his eighth house (other's values). This indicated a problem between how he thought of himself and the value that those in authority placed upon him. His Venus resided in his seventh house (personal relationships and cooperative alliances) and ruled his twelfth house. The kinship he thought was present in his professional position was not actually there.

Last but not least, Patton's Uranus in Libra (disruption of the status quo through all to which it relates) squared both his Venus and Saturn. His Uranus resided in his fifth house (creative endeavors) and ruled his ninth house (broader experiences through education, travel, and ideology). This was a strong message of potential difficulty in personal and professional relationships.

This all draws a picture, again and again, that was fraught with potential difficulty, all going back to how Patton communicated and related his ideas. Despite numerous acknowledgments that he should not "shoot off his mouth" and an awareness that this always resulted in negative consequences, he could not, or would not, take responsible control of this part of his character. I believe he could have instead utilized these same astrological configurations, combined with redirecting his quindeciles, to write the quintessential military manifesto.

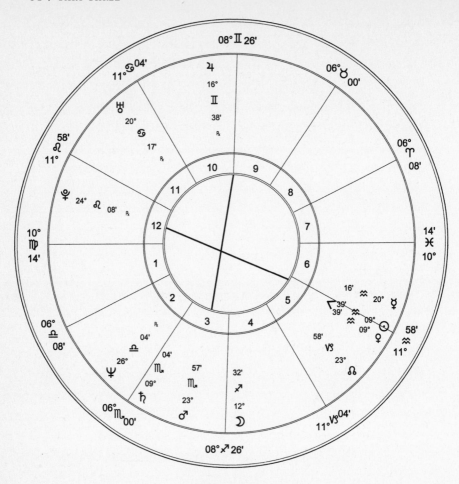

Horoscope 16
Oprah Winfrey / January 29, 1954 / Kosciusko, MS / 7:50 P.M. CST /
(supporting alignments)

Oprah Winfrey has her Pluto in Leo (empowerment or disempowerment through creative self-expression) opposed her Mercury in
Aquarius (use of intelligence and communication through something significant, unusual, and different). Both Pluto and Mercury
square her Mars in Scorpio (application of energy through transformative, regenerative, or controlled means). Mars rules her
eighth house of other's values. Pluto rules her third house (immediate environment and fundamental learning), in which Mars re-

sides. Mercury resides in her sixth house (service, health, the work-place, and relationships with coworkers) and rules her Ascendant (the outer personality) and Midheaven (external focus through career and societal position). It is through this intense application of her energy in the communication of significant issues and a conscious positive projection in her work that she is held in such high esteem, not only by her professional peers, but by people in general.

This is compounded by her Jupiter in Gemini (excess, expansion, and growth through information and ideas) opposed her Moon in Sagittarius (the emotional need to share philosophies and belief systems). This is a clear indication that a strong development of knowledge, personal beliefs, and opinions that she can share with others is essential to Oprah's emotional well-being. One of the prerequisites to this would be a good education. Jupiter rules her fourth house (home, emotional security, and early nurturing) and her Moon resides in the fourth house, suggesting difficulty in the early development of her life. As we know, her childhood was certainly far from easy, and it was not until she went to live with her father, who emphasized the benefits of and need for a solid education, that her life began to turn around. Her Jupiter resides in her tenth house (career and social standing), which indicates a need to focus expanses of knowledge in her profession. Again, without the benefit of education she would not have been able to turn her life around.

Oprah's Saturn in Scorpio (responsibility and authority transformation, regeneration, or control) squares her Sun and Venus in Aquarius (recognition, kinship, and collaboration sought through doing something significant, unusual, and different). Saturn resides in her third house (immediate environment and fundamental learning) and rules her fifth house (creative endeavors), with her Sun residing in that house and ruling her twelfth house (karma, self-undoing, unconscious impulses, and spiritual connection). We know that until she went to live with her father, who in own her words "was a strict disciplinarian," Oprah was already on a path in life that would have led her to even more difficult times. This was the push to which she responded when she finally took control of her own life and became responsible for how the rest of it turned out. Had she not accepted that challenge, the authority that would have taken control of her life would have come from outside, most likely in the form of some kind of oppression. Instead, the reality today is that she is one of the most respected people in the media and openly promotes the necessity for a spiritual connection in one's life.

There are additional configurations in her horoscope that could be referenced, but I think you get my point.

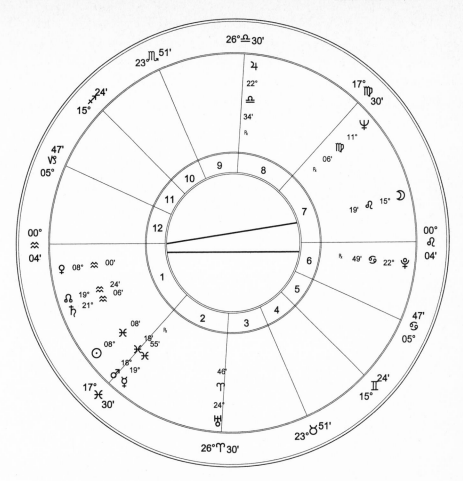

Horoscope 17
Ralph Nader / February 27, 1934 / Winsted, CT / 4:52 A.M. EST

Ralph Nader was, and still is, a public interest activist and the common person's consumer advocate. He first came to America's attention in the 1960s by taking on the automobile industry, which was marketing and selling cars with full knowledge of problems that could and would cause completely preventable deaths. This fight eventually led to landmark consumer safety legislation. He has founded numerous public awareness and consumer rights organizations and has authored many books focusing attention on the rights of citizens and taxpayers in relation to the judicial system, government, and corporate America.

Nader was introduced, at an early age, to the concepts of injustice and inequity in the American system by his immigrant father who was well-known for voicing his opinions about anything and everything. He had already been inside the local courthouse, watching all the action and hearing all the legal wrangling, by the age of four. At fourteen he became a daily reader of the *Congressional Record*. He won a scholarship to Princeton where he began his life calling through his refusal to dress like everyone else and his protests about the university spraying the campus trees with DDT. From Princeton he went on to Harvard Law School where he first became interested in death and injuries caused by automobiles. Upon graduation from Harvard, he opened his own law offices, which quickly became a source of free legal advice for the poor.

At the age of thirty, in 1964, he took his campaign for automobile safety and manufacturer accountability to Washington, D.C. In November of 1965, his first book, *Unsafe at Any Speed: The Designed-in Dangers of the American Automobile*, was published. His efforts as a safety and consumer advocate in relation to the automobile industry culminated in the passage of the Traffic Safety Act, which took effect in 1968.

Nader's voice of discontent has not only made an impact on the automobile industry, but has filtered into almost all areas of corporate America and our government. Like it or not, he will be heard, and he carries the support and gratitude of millions of people as he fights for a safer and more just America.

Ralph Nader has his Pluto in Cancer (empowerment or disempowerment the family and the people) quindecile his Venus in Aquarius (kinship and collaboration through doing something significant, unusual, and different). That same Pluto also squares both his Uranus in Aries (disruption of the status quo through self-focused means) and his Jupiter in Libra (excess, expansion, and growth through all to which it relates). Pluto rules his Midheaven (external focus through career and societal position). This describes, without a doubt, a thrust to work for the benefit of others, but it must have a personal reward as well. That personal reward is the ability to use the power of his perceptions as a major focus in his life.

In addition, Nader also has his Moon in Leo (the emotional need to creatively express the self) quindecile his Aquarius Ascendant (the outer personality demonstrated through doing something significant, different, or unusual). His Moon opposes his Saturn and his North Node in Aquarius (the life purpose demonstrated through responsibility and authority within doing something significant, different, or unusual.). The Moon rules his sixth house (service, health, the workplace, and relationships with coworkers). We have seen this played out dramatically, as he has played a significant role in the revolution of the entire auto industry.

We must also look at the fact that Nader's Sun in Pisces (recognition sought through sensitivity, intuitiveness, and working with the intangible) opposes his Neptune in Virgo (seeking the illusive, imaginary, and ideal through discernment and assimilation). The Sun rules his seventh house (personal relationships and cooperative alliances). This adds to the mix a "knowing" that if we all work together for the benefit of all, then all is possible. Idealistic? Maybe, but without it would he have taken up so many causes for the benefit of us all?

Last, but not least, Ralph Nader has his Saturn (the demonstration of responsibility and authority) square his Midheaven (the external focus through career and societal position). He felt a responsibility to focus his life on this calling, and I for one am grateful that he followed that calling every time that I get into my car.

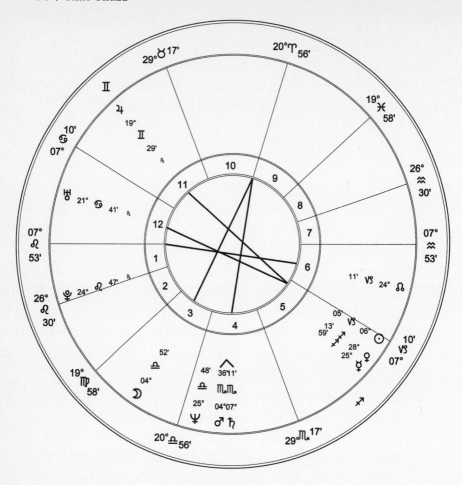

Horoscope 18
Private Case—Jane / December 27, 1953 / Tacoma, WA / 7:02 P.M. PST

Jane, a forty-five-year-old female, came to me for a private consultation because her professional life was unsatisfying and her marriage
had recently ended. She was a corporate lawyer specializing in tax
law at the time of our appointment.

In reviewing Jane's natal horoscope, note that the general placement of the majority of her planets is in the lower hemisphere of
her horoscope, indicating a possible suppression of the ego and
unfinished business stemming from her childhood.

Jane's Moon in Libra (the need to be appreciated) squares her Sun in Capricorn (recognition sought through hard work, ambitions, and goals). The Moon rules her twelfth house (karma, self-undoing, and unconscious impulses), indicating that she may not be aware of the force of her need for appreciation, which could result in problematic situations. Her Sun in Capricorn rules her Leo Ascendant (recognition through the outer personality) focusing her need for approval through her drive for professional recognition. In her attempt to "put her best foot forward," she may in fact end up stepping on others and not even be aware of it.

Jane's Uranus in Cancer (disruption of the status quo within the family) resides in her twelfth house, squares her Aries Midheaven (personal and self-focused drive within career and societal position), and is also quindecile her Sun in Capricorn. Uranus rules her seventh house (personal relationships and cooperative alliances), indicating that unconscious or unresolved disruptions in her early home may fuel her obsession for professional recognition and that they will flow directly into her marriage, partnerships, or cooperative alliances.

In our discussion, Jane informed me that she worked hard (harder than most, according to her) in order to have a secure career and a strong marriage, because her parents divorced when she was five (at which time solar arc Midheaven opposed natal Neptune), and she had vowed she would never let that happen in her own marriage. She further revealed that her mother had not only been the authoritative, dominant parent, but had also been an alcoholic with an erratic temperament. Note that Jane's North Node in Capricorn (the maternal influence focused through hard work, ambitions, and goals) opposes her Uranus in Cancer (disruption of the status quo within the family) in her twelfth house (unconscious impulses and self-undoing) and squares her Neptune in Libra (seeking the ideal, illusive, and intangible through all to which it relates) in her fourth house (home, emotional security, and early nurturing).

Jane's mother died when she was twelve years old (at which time solar arc Neptune was conjunct natal Saturn), and she went to live with her father, who had been a successful businessman who traveled extensively, leaving her alone and in the care of others much of the time. This reinforced the emotional wounding of her Moon in Libra (the need to be appreciated).

Jane focused her adolescent attention on school, working toward good grades and a prime placement at the university of her choice, having decided that a career in law would be where she would make her mark. Note that her Saturn in Scorpio (demonstration of responsibility through control) is conjunct her Mars (applied energy and action), and that they both square her Leo Ascendant (recognition through the outer personality). Mars rules her tenth house (career and social standing) and Saturn rules her sixth house (service, health, workplace, and relationships with coworkers). Her Mars and Saturn are both quindecile her Aries Midheaven (focus through career and societal position). The release from all this tension in her life is focused again and again into her work life and career.

Jane's Mercury is conjunct her Venus in Sagittarius (intelligence, communication, kinship, and collaboration focused through philosophies and belief systems). This combination often creates idealized perceptions. Mercury rules her third house (immediate environment and fundamental learning) and eleventh house (love received), while Venus rules her eleventh house (love received) and fourth house (home, emotional security, and early nurturing). The suggestion here is that through the use of her mind, she may gain reassurance of being loved. She seeks appreciation and approval for her intelligence because of unmet nurturing needs in her early development.

Compounding this is her Moon in Libra (her emotional need to be appreciated) also being quindecile her Aries Midheaven (personal and self-focused drive through career and societal position). Again, her push for approval, recognition, and appreciation will be forceful, indeed. It will be driven through her personality into the arena of her career, perhaps to the point where she is oblivious of everything and everyone else.

During the course of our discussion together, Jane was able to recognize her tendency to use her career as an escape from the emotional difficulties experienced in her early life. She became aware that in her constant efforts to prove herself in her career, she had left very little time or energy to focus on her marriage. She was able to see that her marriage had ended because of her inability to truly share herself in that relationship. She realized that this was a protection against letting herself be vulnerable in case she found that she was not loved or valued by her partner, exactly like she had felt with her father. Jane had never been involved in any kind of professional counseling or therapy to deal with her self-esteem difficulties, and was now ready to begin that process with a view to learning more about herself and how to let herself be trusting and vulnerable in a relationship.

Jane and I also discussed the possibility of refocusing her career from corporate tax law into the area of women's and children's legal issues, with a view to her becoming a champion to those who are less fortunate than herself. This was an area that had always interested her, but she had made the decision early in her career to pursue corporate tax law because it would provide her with a better income.

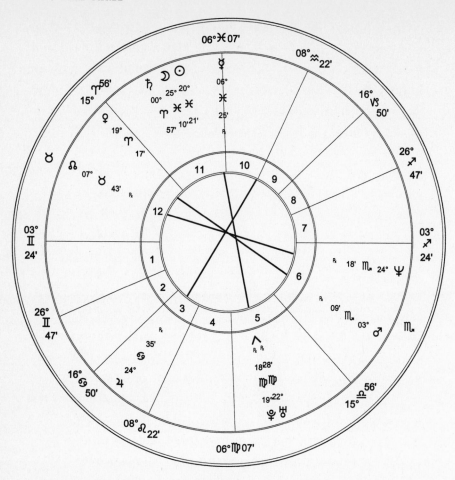

Horoscope 19
Private Case—William / March 11, 1967 / Lansing, MI / 10:05 A.M. EST

William was a young man who came to see me shortly after his thirty-first birthday. He had recently completed a six-month treatment program for alcoholism and drug addiction and was looking for information that, as he put it, "could help him put his life together." He was a high school graduate and had held a series of minimum-wage jobs. He had been involved in petty crime and ended up being arrested, which led to the treatment of his addictions. He now wanted to improve his life and his future prospects.

In reviewing William's natal horoscope, we note that the majority of his planets are focused in the left hemisphere, indicating a strong need for him to be the one to take control of making things happen in his life. There is difficulty suggested in being able to do this because of a dominance of mutable (adjusting and changing) signs contained in his horoscope. This indicates a tendency to become scattered and unable to maintain focus.

There is an enormous thrust of sensitivity indicated by his Moon conjunct his Sun in Pisces (the emotional need to be recognized for sensitivity, intuitiveness, and working with the intangible).

William's Uranus and Pluto in Virgo (assimilation of disruption into empowerment or disempowerment) both oppose his Sun and Moon, intensifying this sensitivity and need for recognition. He is apt to be influenced by everything around him. Uranus rules his Aquarius Midheaven (focus through a different or unique career and societal position) and Pluto rules his sixth house (service, health, workplace, and relationships with coworkers). Is it any wonder that he came with questions regarding the direction of his career?

There is a great deal of tension in any Pluto opposition to the Sun and Moon. It suggests a cloaking of resentment or anger from childhood. William's Sun rules his fourth house (home, emotional security, and early nurturing), confirming this as the origin of the tension. The manifestation of tension is normally demonstrated through anger or frustration. The astrological reference for this is Mars, which in his case is in Scorpio (passionate control) and is retrograde, denoting an inward thrust instead of an outward display of emotion.

During the course of our discussion together, William shared with me his inability to please his father who was verbally abusive toward him during his youth. He was the youngest of five children, with all the rest of his siblings being girls. His father was a loud, strong, "man's" man who loved sports, hunting, wrestling, and truck rallies. William recounted times of intense shame and humiliation because he was never good at any of these things and could not live up to his father's expectations in these areas. His only area of expertise was classical music, which he loved and formally studied until he left home at the age of seventeen, amid fantasies and dreams about becoming a rock star. He rapidly became involved with drugs and alcohol, until eventually they became the sole focus of his life.

William's Jupiter in Cancer (excessive emotional responses) squares his Venus in Aries (kinship and collaboration through self-focused means). Jupiter rules his seventh and eighth houses (relationships, cooperative alliances, and other's values), and Venus rules his twelfth house (karma, self-undoing, and unconscious impulses). This particular combination is suggestive of a tendency to overindulge in whatever feels good at the time in an attempt to escape one's self and feel valued in the company of others.

William has five quindeciles. His Jupiter is quindecile his Aquarius Midheaven (the doing of something big through a unique or different career). His Uranus and Pluto are quindecile his Mercury in Pisces (disruption and empowerment through idealism). His Mars is quindecile his Venus in Aries (self-focused need for kinship drives actions), and his Neptune in Scorpio (the illusion of control) is quindecile his North Node in Taurus (a tangible life purpose) Until our discussion, these quindeciles had played out in his addictions, criminal activity, and an inability to stay focused on any one thing. He had no understanding of how to utilize these dynamics in a harmonious and cooperative effort to work toward something that could be beneficial in his life.

Because of William's tendency to become scattered and unfocused, my suggestion was to direct all of this energy into a structured process of higher education centering around his natural talent and love of music. In order to manifest anything of a tangible nature when one has such a strong mutable focus in the horoscope, it is important that structure is emphasized. His Saturn (demonstration of responsibility and authority) is at the Aries Point (0° of any cardinal sign) and rules his ninth house (higher education and expanded experiences). This suggests his potential to find prominence in a structured educational process.

This suggestion was well received, and when talking with William a year later, I discovered that he was back in school and had remained free of drugs and alcohol.

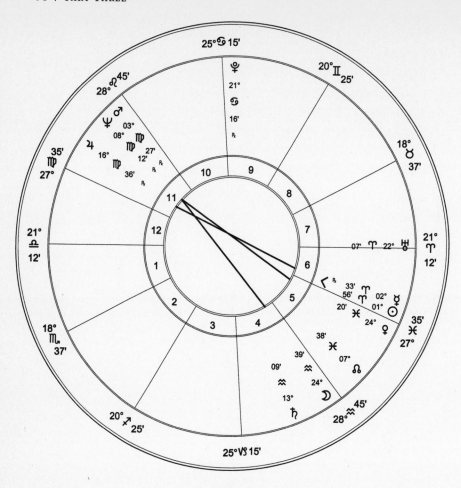

Horoscope 20
Private Case—Sarah / March 22, 1933 / Cambridge, MA / 7:33 P.M. EST

Sarah, a sixty-five-year-old female, came to see me after the death of her husband. She was the mother of three adult children, all of whom lived out of state. She had five grandchildren, but did not see much of them because of difficulties in her relationships with her children. All of them felt that she had been too involved in their lives and now kept their distance except for occasional visits and phone calls. Sarah had never worked and had focused her energy on being the perfect wife and mother. She literally did not know what to do with the rest of her life now that her husband was gone. She came to see if there was some kind of magic answer an astrologer could give her that would suddenly make her life worthwhile again.

In reviewing Sarah's natal horoscope, note that the majority of her planets reside in the right hemisphere. This is an indication of a tendency to live one's life through others. There is also a second suggestion of suppression and unfinished businesses from the early home life indicated by the additional emphasis in the lower hemisphere.

Sarah's Sun is conjunct her Mercury in Aries (idealized perceptions of one's importance). The Sun rules her eleventh house (love received) and Mercury rules her twelfth house (karma, self-undoing, and unconscious impulses). Her need for recognition and love from others will influence her to give up her own needs in order to please others. Both her Sun and Mercury are quindecile her Jupiter in Virgo (excess within assimilation), so this idealized seeking of recognition through others is likely to become a dominant theme in her life.

Sarah's North Node in Pisces opposes her Neptune in Virgo (incorporation and assimilation of an idealized maternal influence and relationship). When I asked her about her relationship with her mother, she informed me that they had always been extremely close. Her mother had even come to live with her shortly after Sarah was married. Her mother had raised her own children by herself, due to the early death of her husband. She had taken in lodgers to make ends meet. She had made sure that all her children had everything they needed and always put their needs well ahead of her own. Sarah and I discussed how much of her life paralleled her mother's life, with the exception of being a widow at a young age. Her Neptune in Virgo (assimilation of the ideal) is also quindecile her Moon in Aquarius (the emotional need to do something significant). Her Moon resides in her fourth house (home and early nurturing) and rules her Cancer Midheaven (external focus through the family and home). This combination suggests that significance comes from her role of wife and mother. Compounding this is her Neptune conjunct her Mars in Virgo (assimilation of the illusion into action), which rules her seventh house (relationships and cooperative alliances). Both Mars and Neptune reside in her eleventh house (love received). Again, the suggestion is reemphasized that Sarah may seek to meet her emotional and physical needs through the role of wife and mother, pushing her to merge her life into the lives of others.

Sarah's Pluto in Cancer (empowerment or disempowerment through the family) rules her second house (self-worth). It conjuncts her Cancer Midheaven (the role of mother) and squares her Libra Ascendant (outer expression of cooperation and harmony). The boost to her self-worth by being the "good wife and mother" is undeniable. Her Pluto squares her Uranus in Aries (disruption of the status quo through self-focused means), which resides in her seventh house (relationships and cooperative alliances) and rules her fifth house (children). Uranus also opposes this same Libra Ascendant. This clearly indicates that any attempt to focus time and attention on her own unique and individual needs could disrupt her role in the family. Again and again, we are brought back to a life focused on meeting the needs of her husband and family well before her own needs.

I suggested to Sarah that she become involved in volunteer activities and charity work to help fill her spare time and give her life more meaning. I emphasized that in doing this she must not continue to make others the entire focus of her life. I also suggested that she join a support group for senior citizens and develop new friendships. I reemphasized a need for her to spend time doing some of the things that she liked but never did because of always having been focused on her husband and children.

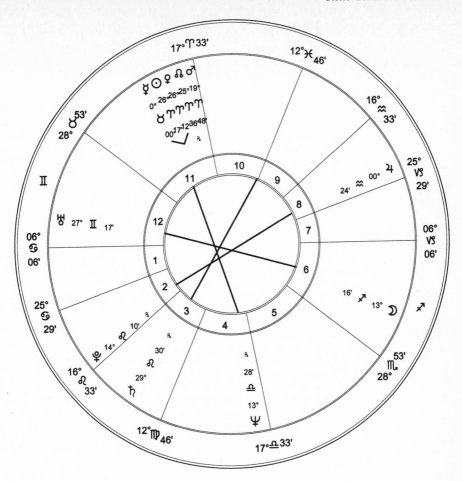

Horoscope 21
Private Case—Jennifer / April 16, 1949 / Toledo, OH / 9:53 A.M. EST

Jennifer, a forty-nine-year-old woman, was a minimum of 150 pounds overweight at the time of our consultation. She was divorced from an abusive husband, with no children, and had worked as a bookkeeper for a small company for the past twenty-five years. Her life consisted of going to work, coming home, and watching television. Her only social activities were occasionally playing Bingo or going to the movies with a friend.

In reviewing Jennifer's natal horoscope, note the pile up of planets contained in her eleventh house (love received), all of which are in the sign of Aries (self-focus) and conjunct each other. Everything in the balance of the horoscope and her life will be influenced by this enormous need for love and recognition.

This powerhouse of energy contains Jennifer's Sun (seeking recognition), Venus (aesthetics, kinship, and collaboration), Mercury (intelligence and communication), Mars (energy applied through action) and North Node (the maternal influence), all in Aries (through self-focused means). Her North Node, Venus, Sun, and Mercury all square her Jupiter in Aquarius (excess within ideas and innovative thought), adding additional tension by magnifying these already dominant needs. Jupiter resides in the eighth house (other's values), which indicates that how much she is valued by others will be what she measures herself by. Her Sun, Venus, and Mercury are all quindecile her Neptune in Libra (seeking the illusive, imaginary, or ideal within all to which it relates). Neptune rules her Pisces Midheaven (external focus through an imaginary, illusive, or idealized career and societal position) and resides in her fourth house (home, emotional security, and early nurturing), suggesting that the origin of her difficulties came from her early home life.

When I asked about her home life, Jennifer revealed to me that her mother had been a wonderful woman and that they had had a good relationship. Note that Jennifer's North Node (the maternal influence) is part of the powerhouse in Aries, and that its closest aspect is with Venus (kinship and collaboration).

She went on to say that her father had been both verbally and physically abusive to all of them. Note that her Saturn in Leo (authority through self-expression) rules her seventh and eighth houses (relationships, cooperative alliances, and other's values). She couldn't get the recognition and love from her father that she needed, so she married someone just like him! Her Saturn is also quindecile her Midheaven (the external focus through the career and societal position), driving her to live up to the messages she received from her father about her role in life. His lack of support created an inability for her to have confidence in herself professionally.

Jennifer's Moon in Sagittarius (the need to have one's opinions respected) squares her Pisces Midheaven and is quindecile her Uranus in Gemini (disruption of the status quo through ideas and information). This is a push to use her mind professionally. The Moon rules her Cancer Ascendant (the outer personality seeking security). The use of her intelligence in her profession needs to bring her the respect she craves. Uranus rules her ninth house (higher learning and expanded experiences) and resides in her twelfth house (karma, self-undoing, and unconscious impulses). In order for her emotional needs to be met, education will not only be important, but essential. When asked about her education level, she informed me that she had left school at the age of fifteen. She had become pregnant and later had a miscarriage (solar arc Midheaven squared natal Uranus at that time). She had obtained a high school equivalency diploma and had taken a few accounting classes at a local college, but had not pursued a degree.

At the time of our consultation, Jennifer had never been involved in any type of therapy or counseling. My suggestion was first to begin a therapeutic process of healing from the difficulties in her early life. We also discussed the possibility of her returning to school to obtain a degree, which would provide her with opportunities to move into a stronger vocational position and thus satisfy her need for respect.

CHAPTER 7

Activation Through Progression and Transit

Times of Obsession and Compulsion

In most cases, time periods of "full-blown" or prominent obsessive-compulsive activity correlate with the alignment of progressed and transiting planets to a natal quindecile configuration. That is not to say that there is no manifestation without activation, but overall it is through stimulation of the tension between the two natal planets in quindecile aspect by outside sources that creates an excessive response. As a general rule, when progressed planets align with a natal quindecile, the introduction of this additional tension will begin to set off a period of heightened sensitivity. Despite the fact that this time frame is stressful and obsessive-compulsive tendencies become a stronger force in the individual's life, it is most often a transiting planet coming into this alignment that sets the whole thing in motion.

With this in mind, I will introduce individual concepts relating to how progressions and transits influence the life direction and manifestation. However, the horoscope examples used will reflect both progressions and transits working together in the same time frame.

Progressions

There are many different methods of progression, and each method is calculated differently. Despite the differences, it is my belief that all progression methods have validity and can provide valuable information. Most astrologers, myself included, have a preferred method of progression that they use as their primary tool for updating natal horoscope information. The intention of this book is not to go into extensive detail on the various methods of progression, because that would take an entire book on its own. To simplify the process, and because of the advantage of easy calculation without the aid of an ephemeris, I will focus this study on the method of progression known as "solar arc direction."

The impact of progressed planets aligning by aspect to the natal quindecile is interesting to watch and the effect can be astounding. Because progressions are a hypothetical movement, it makes sense to me that the manifestation of their impact would normally not come through the outside world ("real world") influences; they would be more prone to internal emphasis in the individual's psyche. Progressed planets tend to heighten the intensity and obviousness of the obsessive-compulsive tendencies. This is done through the nature and characteristics of the progressed planet. For instance, Mercury will intensify the mental processes, so the mind might begin to go over again and again whatever it is dealing with at that time. Progressed Venus will perhaps push the quindecile into the relationship arena or into a need to be with others. Mars will enliven it and push it toward some kind of physical action. For further delineations of the progressed planets, please refer to the last section of this book.

The impact or manifestation of the quindecile comes as a direct result of the "natural" outcome of the ongoing focus that the quindecile has placed on the individual's life, in relation to how aware the individual is of its existence and relevance.

Repetition Factor Through Solar Arc Directions

It is interesting to note that at approximately the age of thirty, through the accumulated movement of solar arc-directed planets, one of the "legs" of a natal quindecile will become aligned again in a second (or repetitive) quindecile with the other "leg" of the natal configuration. For instance, if there is a natal quindecile between Mars at 3° Leo and the Sun at 18° Aquarius, then through solar arc direction the planet Mars will reach 3° Virgo when the individual is approximately thirty years of age. The arc (or space) between 3° Virgo and 18° Aquarius is 165°. Thus we have a second, repetitive quindecile between the original birth planets.

It appears that this is a particularly sensitive time in the manifestation potential of the natal quindecile. Many times the activation of the natal quindecile by this "repetitive" aspect will be the "turning point" of accumulated obsessive-compulsive activity. There can be full-blown activity in the area of life affected, separating the individual totally from the balance of life, thus bringing the issue into the forefront. Interestingly enough, this particular timing can also be the point at which, if the individual has been focusing the natal obsessive-compulsive predisposition into certain goals or objectives, those areas of life may be realized.

Transits

It is my belief that during the times when transiting planets are stimulating natal planets, we have an opportunity to focus our activities toward what we ultimately desire from life, thus utilizing the intense push that is felt from this configuration to keep us motivated and moving toward our goals.

If a transiting planet creates a quindecile to a natal planet, and it is not setting off or stimulating a natal quindecile configuration, the resulting impact will not be prominently felt in the individual's overall life development. That is not to say that there will be no impact at all. There may be periods of obsessive-compulsive tendency, relating to the characteristics of the planets involved. These, however, will not be of the same magnitude as will be demonstrated when an alignment occurs to preconditioned obsessive-compulsive inclinations resulting from a natal quindecile or some other obsessive-compulsive natal indicator.

Progression and Transit Examples

When we take the time periods of increased stimulation through progressed planets aligning with a natal quindecile, and compound them with the introduction of a transiting planet thrusting additional energy into the picture, the tension demanding manifestation is undeniable.

> *Liberace,* with his glorious display of attire and millions of devoted maternal fans, had his Venus in Cancer quindecile his Moon in Sagittarius (use of aesthetics and kinship with the family and people to meet emotional need to express one's philosophies and beliefs). At the time, when Liberace first began to emphasize his "style" through the use of his candelabra and increasingly flamboyant clothing, solar arc-directed Mars (applied energy and action) was opposing his natal Moon. During this same time, transiting Jupiter (excess, expansion, and growth) was squaring his Moon. It had become painfully clear to Liberace that he needed to do something that would connect him to his audience and make him memorable. It was then that the "Liberace" we all remember was born.

> *George Wallace,* governor of Alabama during the height of tension regarding racial integration in our society, will always be remembered for his passionate stand to keep Alabama segregated. Wallace had his Uranus in Aquarius (disruption of the status with something significant, unusual, and different) quindecile his Mercury in Leo (communication through creative self-expression). In 1963, his vision of becoming a national leader was in the process of disappearing when he publicly announced, for the first time, the views and opinions for which he will always be re-

membered. At that time, solar arc-directed Mars (applied energy and action) was quindecile his natal Uranus, and transiting Saturn (the demonstration of responsibility and authority) was opposing his natal Mercury. Opposing racial integration provided him with a platform that made him a political force that could not be denied.

Joseph Mengele, known as the "Angel of Death" for having performed cruel and painful pseudoscientific experiments on inmates of Nazi concentration camps, had his Sun in Pisces quindecile his Moon in Libra (ego's need for recognition in working with the intangible meets the primary emotional need of being appreciated). He also had his Uranus (disruption of the status quo through the use of innovative ideas) quindecile his Cancer Ascendant (the outer personality shown through the family and the people). At the time of his appointment as chief physician at Birkenau and Auschwitz, his solar arc-directed Sun (seeking recognition) was making a repetitive quindecile to natal Moon, and solar arc Ascendant (the outer personality) was making a repetitive quindecile to natal Uranus. At the same time, transiting Jupiter (excess, expansion, and growth) was making a quindecile to natal Uranus. One must remember, when looking at this particular horoscope, that Mengele truly believed that he was doing a positive thing for the future of his family and the German people. It goes without saying that he was terribly mistaken in this belief, but is it any wonder that his experimental concepts and ideas went overboard at this time?

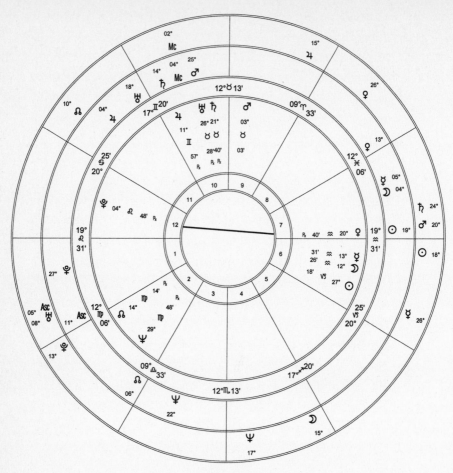

Horoscope 22
Inner ring—Natal Chart—Muhammad Ali / January 17, 1942 /
Louisville, KY / 6:35 P.M. CST
Middle ring—Solar Arc Directions / February 7, 1964 / Louisville, KY /
6:35 P.M. CST
Outer ring—Transits / February 7, 1964 / Louisville, KY /
6:35 P.M. CST

Muhammad Ali, born Cassius Marcellus Clay, was, and in the eyes of many fans always will be, the heavyweight boxing champion of the world. He is the only man in the history of boxing to win this title three times. He is one of boxing's most colorful individuals, and has definitely left an indelible mark on this sport forever.

His amateur fight career began with the winning of six Kentucky Golden Glove and two National Golden Gloves championships and culminated in his winning a gold medal at the 1960 Rome Olympics at the age of 18. Ali then made the decision to go professional and quickly became known not only for his incredible boxing talent, but also for his flamboyant, sharp-tongued, rhyming jibes focused on deriding and mocking his opponents. At the height of his career, just after winning the heavyweight championship for the first time, Ali changed his name and converted to the Islamic religion. Three years later he refused induction into the U.S. Army for religious reasons and was stripped of his heavyweight title and convicted of draft evasion. His fights then took place in the courts instead of in the boxing ring. The U.S. Supreme Court overturned his conviction in 1971, and he went on to regain and defend his heavyweight title.

Where did all the focus that it took to become heavyweight champion and a paragon of conviction come from? When looking at his horoscope I don't see much fire, and the only thing in a cardinal sign (which denotes taking action) is his Sun in Capricorn (recognition sought through hard work, ambition, and tangible goals). He could have applied this to almost any career, so why did he choose boxing, and why are religion and spirituality such a focus in his life?

Muhammad Ali was born at a time when, because of our societal views regarding racial limitations, there were few opportunities for a black man to "make his mark" except through sports. He always knew that he had a strong destiny in life, and boxing provided an opportunity for him to fulfill, what he thought, was that destiny. As a young man he was strong, quick, and full of confidence. He "knew" he was a winner!

Muhammad Ali has his Pluto in Leo (empowerment or disempowerment through creative self-expression) quindecile his Venus in Aquarius (kinship and collaboration through doing something significant, unusual, and different). He certainly had his own perspectives, and his little rhymes were definitely very creative ("Float like a butterfly and sting like a bee . . ."), but what does that have to do with boxing and/or a spiritual emphasis in life?

Ali's Moon and Mercury in Aquarius (an emotional need to communicate something significant, unusual, or different) square (tension creating crisis) his Midheaven (external focus through career and societal position). This suggests a need to succeed and be known somehow, someway. Ali's Mars in Taurus (application of the physical) squares his Sun in Capricorn. Pluto also opposes that same Sun. He knew that he had to do something to become successful in life and his avenue to that was the utilization of his physical energy and strength. He devoted his life, at that time, to that end, and did so superbly. However, I, and many other people, believe that it was Muhammad Ali's taking a powerful stand regarding his religious convictions that made him a "winner" in life, and that this far outweighs all he did in the boxing ring.

In February 1964, Muhammad Ali became the world heavyweight champion, changed his name, and announced his conversion to the Islamic religion. The announcement of his conversion to the Islamic religion was, I feel, the turning point in his life. In his own words: "I don't have that much value on no heavyweight crown. Times when I did, but that was before I found the religious convictions that I have. I could give up fighting and never look back."[1] He announced his religious conversion on February 7, 1964. At that time, Ali's progressed Sun (seeking recognition) was conjunct his natal Venus and therefore blended into his natal quindecile aspect with Pluto. On the day of his announcement, the transiting Sun (throwing a spotlight) and transiting Mars (taking action) were also at that same placement.

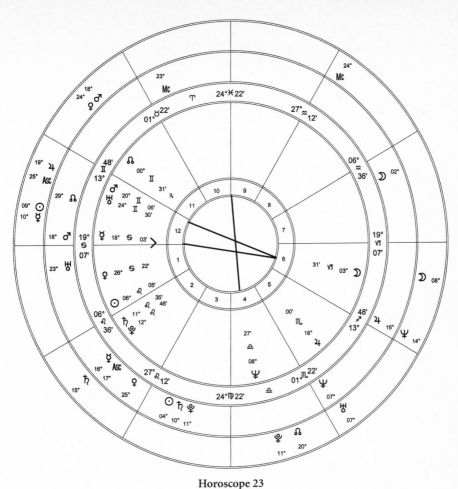

Horoscope 23

Inner Ring—Natal Chart—Arnold Schwarzenegger / July 30, 1947 /
Graz, Austria / 4:10 A.M. CED

Middle Ring—Solar Arc Directions / July 1, 1977 / Graz, Austria /
4:10 A.M. CED

Outer Ring—Transits / July 1, 1977 / Graz, Austria / 4:10 A.M. CED

Arnold Schwarzenegger, action hero and superstar of the 1990s, is
known to us all because of his undeniable appeal in films, making
him the "box office king" of his generation.

Arnold grew up in a small village in Austria. His family was
poor, and his father, being the local constable (policeman), was a

very strict disciplinarian. From the age of thirteen, Arnold would ride the bus into Graz, the closest town of any size, and go to the gym to lift weights. His reward for all that effort was to go to the movie theater and watch adventure movies before returning home.

As he grew into maturity, Arnold won many European body-building titles and the title of Mr. Universe a total of five times. After winning his sixth straight Mr. Olympia title, he announced that he would no longer compete because he wanted to become a movie actor. Everyone told him he was crazy and that he would never be able to accomplish this because of his enormous build and his strange, thick accent.

He studied acting and worked on his english, and in 1977, after having appeared in one minor documentary, he acted in his first somewhat prominent film, *Pumping Iron*. It was at this point that, as Arnold himself has stated, he "became obsessed with the idea of becoming a superstar in the movies."[2]

Arnold has his Moon in Capricorn (the emotional needs met through hard work, ambition, and tangible goals) quindecile his Ascendant and Mercury in Cancer (the outer personality and communication shown through work for the family and the people). His Moon is also quindecile his Mars in Gemini (taking action on ideas and information).

Compounding this is his Neptune in Libra (seeking the illusive, imaginary, and ideal through all to which it relates) quindecile his Pisces Midheaven (sensitivity, intuitiveness, and working with the intangible focused through career and societal position). That is one heck of a lot of obsession and compulsion in one human being. It suggests that he will focus his energies to become successful through that which he shows to others and through some kind of demonstration of that which is not real.

In 1977, with the release of *Pumping Iron*, his progressed Mars (applied energy and action) was making a repetitive quindecile to natal Moon. His progressed Midheaven (the external focus through career and societal position) was also making a repetitive quindecile to natal Neptune, and his progressed Moon was making a third repetitive quindecile to natal Mercury. The tension of these three repetitive alignments must have been enormous.

At the same time, transiting Jupiter (excess, expansion, and growth) was making a quindecile to his already hypersensitized natal Moon. It is no wonder that Arnold focused his life, at that time, on a path that would take him to the heights of stardom and world renown.

CHAPTER 8

Synastry

Synastry is the integration and assimilation of individual elements into a unified component. Applying this to the life of a relationship between two people is a very complex process. As individuals, we are each created with our own unique personalities, emotional needs, personal likes and dislikes, goals and aspirations, and so on. When entering into a relationship with another human being, we are faced with the challenge of finding ways in which to combine and synthesize our personal qualities and yet be able to remain differentiated and an individual in the process.

When incorporating the life energies (i.e., horoscope planetary placements) of one individual into the reality of another, we find that there are areas of compatibility and ease, along with areas of incompatibility and conflict. The arc, or measurement, of one person's planet to a second person's planet will reference how these individual characteristics will express themselves in relation to each other.

Being in a relationship is a primary focus of our lives and our society. Some of this focus comes from nature's requirement for us to "meet, mate, and procreate" in order to perpetuate the species. Some of it comes from our own emotional need to bond with other human beings, and some of it comes from the societal dictates of the particular era in which we live. At any rate, even though it may appear that society as a whole is obsessed with the issue of relationships, it is the individual function or dysfunction in relationships that we need to consider.

If planets are in quindecile aspect in the synastry of two horoscopes, it is an indication that there may be obsessive-compulsive inclinations in that relationship. The extent and nature of those tendencies will be referenced through the dynamics and personal importance of the planets involved; however, the inclination will not be nearly as powerful if the individuals involved do not have quindeciles in their own natal horoscopes. If person *A* has natal quindeciles and person *B* doesn't, the obsession-compulsion in the relationship may be one-sided, with person *A* focusing on person *B*. If both people have natal quindeciles and there are quindeciles through the synastry of the two horoscopes, the dynamics of the relationship may be overwhelmingly obsessive-compulsive.

Prince Charles' natal Neptune and Venus in Libra are quindecile his Moon in Taurus (an emotional need to collaborate in relating to the ideal in a tangible manner through all to which it relates). Camilla Parker Bowles' Jupiter in Scorpio is quindecile her North Node in Gemini (transformation and regeneration on a grand scale through recognition and renown resulting from information). It has been interesting to watch her public persona shift from the evil "other woman" to an acceptable partner for Charles. When combining these two horoscopes through synastry, we find Camilla's Jupiter in Scorpio is quindecile Charles' Moon and North Node in Taurus (transformation and regeneration on grand scale meeting tangible emotional need focused in the life path). It makes me wonder if these two people were destined to be together, but because of circumstances they got off track and have now come back to the course intended.

John Lennon's natal Uranus in Taurus is quindecile his Mercury in Scorpio (communication of transformative ideas disrupts the status quo). Yoko Ono's natal Mars in Virgo is quindecile her Sun in Aquarius (applied action toward assimilation of the ego's need for recognition of doing something significant). When combining these two horoscopes through synastry, we find that John's Uranus in Taurus is quindecile Yoko's Moon in Sagittarius (disruption of the status quo through tangible demonstration of philosophies and belief systems to meet the emotional need). Yoko's Pluto in Cancer is quindecile John's Midheaven in Capricorn (perspectives of the family and people focused through ambition and tangible goals). Surely this must be the "love in" demonstrations they held together in bed, while holding press conferences about their views on "make love not war."

The United States has natal Pluto in Capricorn quindecile the Sun in Cancer (the ego of the people recognized through the power of hard work and ambition). Israel has natal Jupiter in Sagittarius quindecile Mercury in Gemini (expanded beliefs through ideas and information). When combining these two horoscopes through synastry, we find that Israel's Moon in Leo is quindecile the U.S.'s Moon in Aquarius (emotional needs common to both are expressed and recognized through the doing of something significant). Israel's Pluto in Leo is quindecile the U.S.'s Pluto in Capricorn (the power of shared perspectives expressed and through hard work and ambition), and Israel's Mars in Leo is quindecile the U.S.'s Aquarius Midheaven (taking creative actions within the societal position of doing something significant). Is it any wonder that our ties are so strong with the nation of Israel?

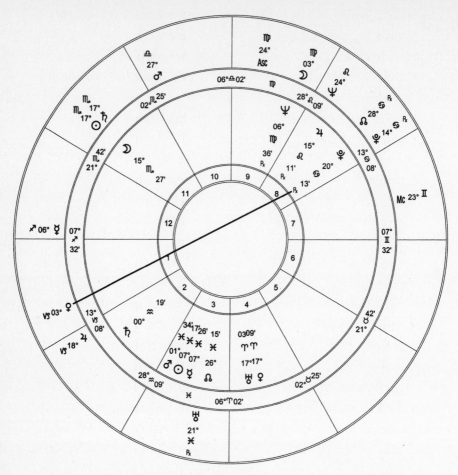

Horoscope 24
Inner Chart—Elizabeth Taylor / February 27, 1932 / London, England /
2:00 A.M. GMT
Outer Chart—Richard Burton / October 10, 1925 / Pontrhydyfen, Wales /
2:30 A.M. GMT

Elizabeth Taylor and Richard Burton had an obsessive-compulsive
relationship that covered the front pages of newspapers and maga-
zines throughout the world.

In Elizabeth Taylor's natal horoscope, her Jupiter in Leo (excess
within self-expression) is quindecile both her Mars in Pisces (applied action within sensitivity, intuitiveness, and working with the

intangible) and her Saturn in Aquarius (responsibility within doing something significant, unusual, and different). Her excessive approach in life has been noted not only in her relationship with Burton, but also through her alcoholism, workaholism, and taking up of the AIDS cause.

In Richard Burton's natal horoscope, his Uranus in Pisces (disruption of the status quo through sensitivity, intuitiveness, and working with the intangible) is quindecile his Moon in Virgo (the emotional need to assimilate and incorporate) This is a strong pull toward becoming totally emersed, to the exclusion of all else, with whatever he is involved with at the time. Thus we have his alcoholism and well-documented workaholism.

When looking at these two horoscopes through synastry, we find that Elizabeth's Pluto in Cancer (empowerment through the perspective of family) is quindecile Richard's Venus in Capricorn (collaboration through hard work, ambition, and goals). Pluto and Venus together in a quindecile aspect is a powerful combination because of the enormous need it focuses on the power of relationship.

It is interesting to note that when Taylor and Burton met, during the filming of *Cleopatra*, they both has progressed and transiting planets accentuating their individual natal quindeciles. Elizabeth Taylor's progressed Saturn (demonstration of ambition) and transiting Jupiter (excess) were both quindecile her natal Jupiter, creating repetitive natal quindeciles. Richard Burton's progressed Jupiter (excess) was quindecile his natal Moon (the emotional need), and transiting Pluto (empowerment or disempowerment through perspectives) was quindecile his natal Uranus (disrupting the status quo), creating a time of hypersensitivity in his natal Uranus-Moon quindecile.

It has been interesting to note that despite all the hard work and energy that went into the making of the film *Cleopatra*, by both of them and by the film industry, it is the relationship between Taylor and Burton that will always be remembered rather than the film itself.

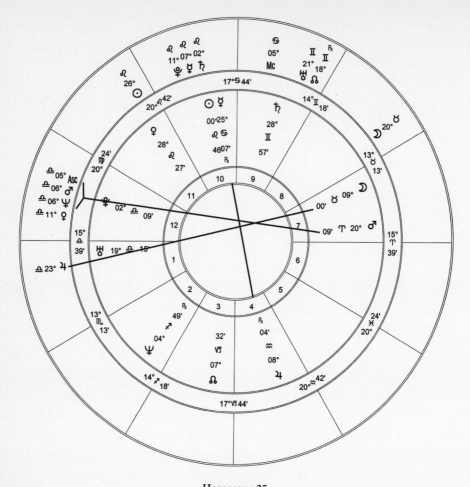

Horoscope 25
Outer Chart—Bill Clinton / August 19, 1946 / Hope, AR /
8:51 A.M. CST
Inner Chart—Monica Lewinsky / July 23, 1973 / San Francisco, CA /
12:21 P.M. PST

Bill Clinton and Monica Lewinsky had an extramarital relationship that was focused on worldwide and very nearly brought down
the American presidency. It was the lead story for the American
press for over a year, despite the fact that there were many more
important issues going on during that time. We were bombarded
with every inappropriate word uttered and every inappropriate act

that occurred during their relationship. I, for one, am thankful that we are finally past this particular issue, and I want to take this opportunity to apologize for feeling the need to utilize this example in this book. The synastry of these two horoscopes is an excellent illustration of a one-sided obsessive-compulsive relationship, though, so with your indulgence, I will continue.

Bill Clinton has absolutely no quindeciles in his natal chart. Granted there are other interesting configurations, some of which even reference addictive or obsessive characteristics, but there are no quindeciles!

Monica Lewinsky, on the other hand, has her Jupiter in Aquarius (excessive need to do something significant, unusual, and different) quindecile her Mercury in Cancer (communication of ideas through the family or people). According to documented accounts, this was not her first obsessive relationship with a married man, which confirms her excessive and unique ideas about the concept of "family."

When we look at these two horoscopes through synastry, we find that four of Bill's astrological placements are quindecile two of Monica's placements. Bill's Ascendant (the outer personality), Mars (the taking of action), and Neptune (a seeking of the illusive, imaginary, and ideal) all in Libra (through all to which it relates) are quindecile Monica's Mars in Aries (the taking of action through personal and self-focused means). This is compounded by Bill's Jupiter in Libra (excessiveness in all to which it relates) quindecile Monica's Moon in Taurus (the emotional need met through something tangible). So, in a nutshell, Bill's influence on Monica stimulated her need to act (Mars) on meeting her emotional needs (Moon).

We must also take into consideration that both Monica's Mars and Moon reside in her seventh house (one-to-one relationships and cooperative alliances), with Mars ruling that same house. Her Moon rules her Midheaven (the external focus through career and societal position). This is an incredible draw to be in a relationship with the person who is stimulating these areas of life. When looking at these two horoscopes, I can understand how and why this relationship happened. It is important to note that the obsession with the relationship was Monica's and not Bill's, and the horoscopes substantiate that.

It is also interesting to note that at the time of the first kiss (the timing of which is readily available through the excessive documentation), Monica's progressed Sun was quindecile her natal Jupiter, stimulating her natal quindecile, with a need for ego recognition. At the same time, transiting Venus was quindecile her natal Saturn (the need to cooperate and collaborate with authority), and the transiting Sun was quindecile her natal Moon (throwing a spotlight on the emotional needs). Thus, we have the onset of the relationship that rocked the presidency.

---

1. See David Remnick, *King of the World: Muhammad Ali and the Rise of an American Hero* (New York, NY: Random House, 1998) 291.

2. See Wendy Leigh, *Arnold: An Unauthorized Biography* (Chicago, IL: Congdon & Weed, Inc., 1990) 176.

PART IV

Index of Quindecile Delineations

This section references various possibilities of potential dynamics within any quindecile combination. Information is also provided that references possible dynamics of a third planetary influence within these combinations.

SUN

Sun–Moon

Sun (seeking of ego recognition) quindecile Moon (the emotional need)—May be completely driven to fulfill one's own emotional needs and focus only on one's self in the process. May seek security through the attainment of recognition. There can be lack of objectivity with this particular pair. May be extremely self-centered and oblivious to the rest of the world. Can be extremely dependent or overly confident and assertive within relationships. Benefit can be found through the development of a strong relationship with one's self.

Sarah Ferguson, David Bowie, Heinrich Himmler

When incorporated with:

Mercury—One's thoughts may become consumed with ideas about how to fulfill one's emotional needs. May become impulsive regarding marriage. This can be very helpful in self-evaluation or therapeutic interaction for emotional healing. Can be beneficial in the communication of ideas.

Venus—The need for relationship may be highlighted. May focus on material security when emotional security is not present. This can be an asset when working toward a healthy basis of self-worth. This can also heighten artistic awareness and creative sensitivity.

Mars—May become ruthless or aggressive in trying to get one's needs met. May anger easily when frustrated. Sexuality may be highlighted. May become pushy, assertive, or aggressive in relationships. Benefits are found by placing one's focus on others and working toward a common goal.

Jupiter—May become overconfident or have an exaggerated sense of self. Can become overly enthusiastic and unrealistic. Belief systems and opinions may be a major part of one's identity. This can be excellent for the development of healthy relationships when adequate education has been received. The sharing of philosophies and belief systems may be beneficial.

Saturn—May have difficulty with relationships because of authoritative stance or difficulty accepting advice and suggestions from others in an authority position. May become driven by ambition. Achievement may become a means to seek recognition. This can be excellent for acceptance of personal responsibility. An asset when utilized toward reaching one's goals.

Uranus—One may be driven by a need to be different. Individuality is highlighted. Relationships may be unpredictable, risky, or disruptive. There may be a prominent need for excitement. This can be utilized to make major changes in one's life. May be a trendsetter or take the lead in influencing societal changes.

Neptune—Idealism, addictions, and escapism may be prominent. Relationship codependency may be highlighted. May have great insight and an ability to develop strong spiritual relationships. May possess artistic sensitivity and creative self-expression.

Pluto—Manipulation, control, and an overbearing personality may be present. May be forceful and aggressive in getting one's needs met. There is excellent opportunity for self-awareness through deep evaluation or therapeutic processes. Major possibility for success and prominence.

North Node—May be thrust into prominence. The maternal relationship may be intensely involved in one's inner and outer development. One's life purpose may be highlighted. Developing new associations is important in one's life.

Ascendant—Emotional security and ego recognition may be sought through social interaction. One may focus only on one's self within relationships. Narcissism or codependency may be present within the personality. There are positive results when using this to work and share with others. Others are helpful in the redirection and refocus of one's life.

Midheaven—May become obsessed regarding one's career and societal position. Marriage may be used to promote one's own agenda. Personal needs may be met through ego recognition. This can be very beneficial in attainment of success or setting goals for self-development.

Sun–Mars

Sun (seeking of ego recognition) quindecile Mars (application of energy in the form of action)—May use physical energy and action to gain recognition, prove one's self, and build the ego. Can be

strongly competitive and aggressive. May have lots of sexual energy. Excellent ability to accomplish goals if aggressiveness is turned into assertiveness and energy is focused and directed.
James Dean

When incorporated with:

Mercury—May impulsively act on what one thinks. Can become consumed with ideas and schemes to gain recognition. May have a tendency to take on too many projects at one time. Benefit comes through evaluating one's ego needs and personal desires and taking steps to meet them.

Venus—Relationship needs and issues can be strongly heightened. The urge for romance or affairs may be present. Material gain and financial security may be actively sought. Artistic expression and creativity can be accentuated. Benefit comes by developing self-worth through actions taken in life.

Jupiter—May have an exaggerated need to justify one's actions. Need for ego recognition may be exaggerated. May take on too many projects. Overindulgence in sexual activity can be present. Benefit comes through educational pursuits and the building of philosophies and beliefs.

Saturn—May constantly take on additional responsibility to prove one's self. Workaholism may be present. Can be authoritative, overbearing, and aggressive. Benefit comes through setting goals in one's life and acting on them.

Uranus—May possess an impulsive temperament, and explosions may come "out of the blue." Individuality and doing things one's own way may be emphasized. Love of excitement and taking risks may be prominent. Unusual or impulsive sexual activity may result. May feel a need to lead revolutionary causes. Benefit comes through focusing on individuality to make changes in one's life. May possess creative or artistic talents.

Neptune—May get caught in the pursuit of the ideal, dream, fantasy, or illusion. Addictions may be prominent. May act through deceit. Benefit comes through pursuit of spiritual development. May possess artistic or creative abilities.

Pluto—Pursuit of power and prestige can be highlighted. Use of control, manipulation, or abuse can be prominent. Benefit comes through pursuit of internal investigation into one's own psyche.

North Node—May be thrust into recognition or renown for actions taken. The maternal relationship may be aggressive or may have taught one how to be assertive. Benefit comes through working on projects that benefit others.

Ascendant—Need for recognition from others can drive actions taken. May do anything to get noticed. May be aggressive and ruthless. Pursuit of relationships may be prominent. Benefit comes by using physical energy to help others.

Midheaven—Can be driven by self-promotion through one's career. May push one's authority on others. May marry impulsively to get ahead. Benefit comes through setting goals and working toward reaching them.

Sun–Jupiter

Sun (seeking of ego recognition) quincecile Jupiter (excess, expansion, and growth)—May be driven to obtain fame, recognition, reward, and success. Can be opinionated, judgmental, and egocentric. Excess and indulgence may be prominent. Everything is not enough. "I am the greatest!" mentality. Can have king/queen complex. Must utilize ongoing education to support the ego and manifest possible potentials within one's life.
Fred Astaire, Red Skelton

When incorporated with:

Mercury—May be obsessed with grandiose ideas and schemes to get ahead. May take on too many projects at one time. Benefit comes through educational pursuits and development of one's mind.

Venus—Relationships can be obsessive. May measure success and self-worth through material gain. Overindulgence may be prominent. Beneficial when working for the benefit of others and sharing personal resources.

Saturn—May be excessively authoritative. Ambitions may take center stage to gain ego recognition. May push to prove one's point. Beneficial for positive and realistic goal setting. May assume a position of authority within expression of philosophies and belief systems.

Uranus—Intense need for excitement can promote risk taking. Can intensify demonstration of one's individuality. May think the law doesn't apply to one's self. Benefit comes through changing old opinions and beliefs through innovative ideas and educational processes.

Neptune—Obsession, addictions, and escapism can be prominent. May have idealized perceptions of one's self. May become overly involved in pursuit of one's beliefs. Benefit comes through pursuit of spiritual concepts. Intuition may be strong. Sensitivity within creative self-expression is highlighted.

Pluto—May be driven to obtain power and success. May force one's own agenda on others because of a need to be right. Benefit comes through therapeutic education to understand and transform one's life.

North Node—May be thrust into renown because of one's belief systems. The maternal influence may be emphasized. Benefit comes through educational pursuits that focus on the development of one's life purpose.

Ascendant—Recognition needs may be overly emphasized. May use one's success to impress others or to gain advantage within relationships. May focus on relationships with others because of common belief systems, opinions, or educational pursuits. Benefit comes through sharing ideas and knowledge with others.

Midheaven—The drive for recognition may be sought through one's career or societal position. Belief systems, opinions, and biases can be on display. Benefit comes through working toward goals that are beneficial not only to one's self, but also to others. Has the potential for becoming a leader within philosophical development or promotion of belief systems.

Sun–Saturn

Sun (seeking ego recognition) quindecile Saturn (demonstration of responsibility or authority)—May be obsessed with self-doubt and a need to "measure up." May take on too much responsibility or may not accept responsibility at all. Can be driven to prove one's self through accomplishments and ambitions. Can be cold and calculating. May assume authoritative role with others. Father or authoritative parent may be a major influence. Needs to become one's own authority. Can set goals and accomplish them if focused and directed. *Marlon Brando, Nancy Kerrigan, Nostradamus*

When incorporated with:

Mercury—May be prone to depression and self-doubt. May use calculation and strategy to get ahead. Fear of inadequacy may be prominent. Benefit comes through understanding ego difficulties. Can set goals and accomplish them, especially when directed toward achievement of ambitions.

Venus—Relationships may be used to gain recognition. May marry an authority figure. Self-esteem difficulties may be prominent. Fear of inadequacy or not being loved may be present. Benefit comes through working to establish a strong sense of self-worth. May have the ability to work well with financial matters.

Uranus—May be driven to rebel against feelings of inadequacy and restriction. May decide to change one's career course repeatedly. May clash with authority. Benefit comes through changing old patterns that deny the personal use of one's authority. Can be instrumental in changing outdated concepts within society.

Neptune—Escapism, addictions, and workaholism may be used to avoid one's fears and feelings of inadequacy. May fear or run away from responsibility. May fear authority. May abuse position of authority. Benefit comes through setting spiritual goals and working toward them.

Pluto—May assert one's authority in a manipulative manner. Power and control over others may be used to gain recognition. May become overpowered by feelings of inferiority. Benefit comes through setting goals to heal one's wounded psyche.

North Node—Renown may come through assumption of a leadership role. Mother may have been the authoritative parent. Benefit comes through working with others to reach a common goal.

Ascendant—Reserved and controlled personality may be prominent. May possess a strong drive to get one's achievements noticed by others. May take the authoritative role in relationships. Benefit comes through working with others toward a common goal and setting the personal goal to trust others.

Midheaven—Career focus may be all-consuming. May seek a position of authority. Marriage may be used to gain recognition. Benefit comes through setting goals to develop self-confidence. May assume a public leadership role.

Sun–Uranus

Sun (seeking of ego recognition) quindecile Uranus (disruption of the status quo through unique and innovative ideas)—May be driven by a need for constant excitement and stimulation. May be a rebel. A need for independence and individuality can be prominent. May have a sense of mission in needing to be different. May feel that "the rules don't apply to me"! May live on the edge. May take up a "cause" and work for humankind in some significant way. *Catherine the Great, Lucille Ball, Luciano Pavarotti*

When incorporated with:

Mercury—May have erratic thinking and act impulsively on ideas. Can become consumed by outrageous ideas and schemes to gain ego recognition. May shock others through one's use of communication. Benefit comes from understanding how to break free from old patterns of behavior. Can be good at brainstorming. Can be brilliant with innovative concepts and unique perspectives.

Venus—May become involved in affairs or risky relationships. May have difficulty with long-term relationships because of a need for excitement. Self-worth may be based on being different and unique. Can be financially irresponsible and unpredictable. Benefit comes by developing self-worth and personal style through appreciation of own individuality. Can be extremely creative and avant garde.

Neptune—Loss of identity may drive one's need to rebel. Confusion and unrealistic expectations may be prominent. Benefit comes through development of unique and individual spiritual concepts. Artistic and creative expression is highlighted. Can become involved in major shifts in consciousness of the times.

Pluto—The need for recognition of one's individuality may be magnified. May be driven to seek power through unconventional means. May use shock or surprise to gain the upper hand. Benefit comes through making transformative changes in one's life. May become involved in societal shifts and rebellions.

North Node—Recognition from others for one's individuality may come "out of the blue." The maternal relationship may be disruptive, unpredictable, or unconventional. Benefit comes through working with others toward a common cause.

Ascendant—May be driven by a need to show others how unique and different one can be. May need to be seen as a trendsetter. Constant changes of location may occur. Benefit comes through working with others toward a common cause.

Midheaven—Constant change of direction in one's career may be prominent. May defy authority. May use marriage to shock others or to become independent. May be driven to shock society at large. May become a leading influence within societal change.

Sun–Neptune

Sun (seeking of ego recognition) quindecile Neptune (seeking the illusive, imaginary, and ideal)—May live in illusion, fantasy, and deception. May lack self-confidence and a sense of identity. May see one's self as a victim or become a martyr. Feelings of powerlessness may drive one's personality. Addictions and indulgences can be prominent. Can have great artistic sensitivity, creativity, and expression. May have strong intuition and insight.
H. G. Wells, Paul Newman, Quincy Jones

When incorporated with:

Mercury—Idealized and unrealistic perceptions may be highlighted. One's thoughts can be consumed with ideas of fantasy, romance, and illusion. May be unable to communicate in concrete and realistic terms. Benefit comes through utilization of meditation and development of spiritual concepts. May be extremely intuitive and artistically sensitive.

Venus—Codependency and idealization of relationships may be highlighted. May focus entirely on one's partner instead of on one's self. May use deceit within relationships. Benefit comes through development of self-worth. Creativity is highlighted. Artistic sensitivity can be prominent.

Mars—Idealism, escapism, and addictions may be an active force within one's life. Self-control may not be present. May be abused or abuse others. Benefit comes through taking action toward spiritual development. May instinctively know what needs to be done.

Pluto—May abuse one's power or be deceitful to get ahead. May become obsessed with fantasy. Escapism and addiction can be prominent. Benefit comes through powerful transformation of one's spiritual concepts of life. Can have powerful spiritual perspectives and the ability to live them out. Therapeutic assistance through others can be essential because of a tendency to not see things clearly or objectively.

North Node—Can gain recognition because of one's spiritual focus or artistic sensitivity. Idealization of the maternal relationship may be present. Benefit comes through the use of sensitivity, intuitiveness, and insight within one's life.

Ascendant—May be deceitful in dealing with others. May feel driven to merge with others. Codependency, addictions, and escapism may be present. May sacrifice one's own needs in order to be recognized as someone who is sensitive to others. Benefit comes by working with others toward a universal understanding of peace. Can be artistically sensitive and creative.

Midheaven—Idealistic expectations may drive one's career. Marriage may be used to establish one's identity. May use deceit within one's career or marriage. Escapism and addictions may be prominent. Benefit through use of artistic sensitivity. Structure and realistic goals may be needed to manifest anything.

Sun–Pluto

Sun (seeking of ego recognition) quindecile Pluto (empowerment or disempowerment through perspectives)—May use one's intense drive to gain power and control. Can be focused on prominence and success. Can be ruthless, manipulative, and intimidating. Has ability to transform one's life and perspectives by purging old concepts. Can possess strong strength of character. Self-evaluation and therapeutic processes helpful.

Ivana Trump, J. Paul Getty, Oprah Winfrey

When incorporated with:

Mercury—May be driven by schemes and ideas to gain an advantage. May utilize verbal and mental manipulation to get ahead. Benefit comes from intense self-evaluation. Can possess the ability to communicate powerful perspectives effectively to others.

Venus—May manipulate and control relationships. Monetary gain may be used to gain recognition. May control the purse strings. May have a powerful impact when focusing on helping others. May have powerful artistic expression and style.

North Node—May become renowned for powerful perspectives and/or one's use of power. The maternal influence may be powerful. Benefit comes through the use of powerful perspectives to benefit others. Can regenerate one's self many times within this lifetime.

Ascendant—May use manipulation and control with others or within relationships. May be driven to be seen as someone who is in control or powerful by others. Benefit comes through working with other's perspectives. Can express powerful perspectives to others.

Midheaven—Driven to seek power through success and career. May seek a powerful marriage to gain recognition. Benefit comes through transforming one's life goals periodically. May possess powerful leadership abilities.

Sun–North Node

Sun (seeking of ego recognition) quindecile North Node (the life purpose, recognition and renown, the maternal influence)—May identify one's self through one's mother. Can be driven to feed one's ego through one's public persona. Has the ability to make new contacts easily and network within a "common cause."
Joan Crawford, Uri Geller

When incorporated with:

Mercury—May become known for one's use of communication or intelligence. Ideas and concepts may be influenced through the maternal relationship. Benefit comes by focusing on the use of ideas that benefit others. May have the ability to communicate and present concepts well.

Venus—May become known through one's relationship or monetary gains. May copy maternal modeling within relationships. Benefit comes through sharing with others and building one's self-esteem. A personal sense of style and artistic expression may be present.

Ascendant—May be driven by relationship dependency or a need for social contacts. The maternal influence may be seen through one's physical appearance and personality. Benefit comes by seeking ways to work with others toward a common cause.

Midheaven—Can be obsessed regarding one's professional contacts and career opportunities. May marry to gain recognition. The maternal influence may be demonstrated through one's career choice. Benefit comes from setting goals and working to achieve them.

Sun–Ascendant

Sun (seeking of ego recognition) quindecile Ascendant (the outer personality)—May be driven to be recognized through one's external appearance. "You will notice me!" attitude. Ego may be tied to other people's responses. May be driven to be the center of attention. Relationships may be a focus. Benefit comes through working with others to gain self-awareness.

Katharine Hepburn, Charles Manson

When incorporated with:

Mercury—Can be driven to impress others through one's communication or mental abilities. May talk incessantly. May push one's ideas onto others to gain recognition. Benefit comes from understanding others. Can possess excellent communication skills.

Venus—May actively pursue material gain or relationships to obtain recognition from others. May be driven to be seen as beautiful in physical appearance. Benefit comes by working with others. Can possess an artistic and creative style.

Midheaven—May be driven to succeed through one's career. Prominence and societal position may be a focus. May marry for recognition. Benefit comes through setting goals and working to achieve them. May become successful simply by being one's self.

Sun–Midheaven

Sun (seeking of ego recognition) quindecile Midheaven (external focus through one's career and societal position)—May be driven toward fame, success, and ego recognition. Can be driven to take center stage. May have the ability to set goals and reach them realistically, taking into account ego needs, talents, and so on. May be artistic and creative.

Allen Ginsberg, Christian Dior, Ivana Trump

Moon

Moon–Mercury

Moon (the emotional need) quindecile Mercury (use of intelligence and communication)—Emotional responses may drive the thought processes, methods of communication, and speech patterns. One must express one's feelings. Emotional immaturity may be highlighted. Intuition and insight may be prominent. Excellent for self-evaluation when objectivity is present. Has the potential to convey ideas in a caring, intuitive manner and works well with other people.

L. Ron Hubbard, Red Skelton, Luciano Pavarotti

When incorporated with:

Venus—May focus obsessively on relationships or the attainment of financial security. May become overly emotional when dealing with others. This is beneficial when working on self-esteem and personal values. Can be extremely artistic and creative.

Mars—May be verbally aggressive or abusive when emotions are heightened. May be focused on doing what one thinks is needed, regardless of possible consequences. Active participation in working toward emotional understanding is beneficial. Can be helpful in being assertive when sharing feelings, information and ideas with others.

Jupiter—May have grandiose, lofty, or unrealistic ideas. Can be excessively opinionated. Emotionally driven responses may be out of proportion to the situation. This can be useful for developing personal philosophies or belief systems. Success within pursuit of one's educational goals and use of emotional expression and communication.

Saturn—May be emotionally inhibited and reluctant to express one's feelings. Depression may be prominent. Relationships may become oppressive, or one may take the authoritative role with others. Workaholism may be a factor. May assume too much responsibility because of trust issues with others. Benefit comes through an ability to set and realize one's goals and ambitions.

Uranus—Can be obsessed with a need for independence. May feel a need to "live on the edge." Taking risks and chances is highlighted. May have a tendency to shock others through one's communication and ideas. Excellent for problem solving, brainstorming, and making changes in one's life to disrupt old patterns of emotional response.

Neptune—May be overly idealistic in perception of one's self. May be unconscious of abusive or addictive behaviors. Can have unrealistic expectations. May be the martyr in relationships. Can be extremely sensitive within artistic expression and creative endeavors. Benefit comes through strong spiritual development.

Pluto—May be emotionally manipulative and controlling. Emotional perspectives may be pushed to the forefront. May be ruthless and intimidating when sharing ideas and information with others. Powerful emotional perspectives can be prominent. Communication and writing can have a major impact on others. Benefit comes through self-awareness through deep and probing self-evaluation. There is an ability to purge old concepts and transform emotional perspectives.

North Node—Relationships may be accentuated. Emotional responses may be influenced by the maternal relationship. May be thrust into a position of prominence. The sharing of emotional perspectives with others can be beneficial in understanding one's life purpose.

Ascendant—May push one's emotional perspectives on others. May be obsessed with actively seeking relationships. May be overly emotional with others and wear one's feelings on one's sleeve. Can be beneficial when allowing others to assist in one's journey of self-understanding. Can emotionally relate with others and use communication abilities successfully.

Midheaven—Security through one's career and recognition from authorities may be a strong focus. May marry to gain position or social acceptance. Emotional responses may be on display. Benefit can be found within communication of emotional perspectives within a professional setting. Excellent for setting goals and working toward self-awareness and understanding.

Moon–Venus

Moon (primary emotional need) quindecile Venus (the need to co-operate and collaborate)—May seek security through either love or money. Can be prone to self-indulgence. Possible eating disorders or addictions. May tend to "mother" or smother one's partner. Value and self-esteem may be linked to one's charm and beauty. Can possess a wonderful sense of beauty and artistry. Creativity is strongly highlighted. Relationships with others can be caring and nurturing.

Karen Carpenter, Jack Kerouac, Prince Charles

When incorporated with:

Mars—May become pushy or aggressive in relationships because of one's emotional insecurity. May substitute action for feelings. May become overindulgent in an attempt to escape emotional difficulties. This combination may benefit when actively working and sharing with others.

Jupiter—Can promote an exaggerated sense of emotional need. Indulgences and idealism may become full-blown. Addictions may be present. Can be excellent for developing personal belief systems that support one's life. Benefit comes through personal education. Artistic sensitivity and an enormous sense of beauty can be present.

Saturn—May withdraw from relationships because of a fear of loss or lack of self-esteem. May take on excessive responsibility in order to feel valued. May take the authority position within relationships. Benefit comes through setting realistic goals that promote a healthy self-esteem. Being responsible for sharing one's emotions is essential in building trust with others.

Uranus—May be drawn toward risky or unconventional relationships. May possess an idealized need for emotional security that cannot be met by others. May disrupt one's relationships on a regular basis. Benefit through making changes in security issues.

Neptune—Idealism, addictions, and escapism may be prominent. Emotional sensitivity is highlighted. Need for relationships may drive one's life. Benefit comes through development of spiritual relationships. Artistic sensitivity and creative self-expression is highlighted.

Pluto—May use manipulation and control to meet one's emotional needs or obtain financial security. May be drawn to partners who will take control. Benefit comes through the sharing of emotional perspectives with others. Can provide opportunity for self-evaluation and transformation of one's life through internal investigation.

North Node—The need for emotional security through others may be prominent. May be thrust into recognition through one's relationships. The maternal relationship may influence one's success or failure within relationships. Benefit can be found through sharing one's emotional needs and perceptions with others.

Ascendant—May become driven by a need for approval and acceptance in social situations. Feelings and emotions may be projected onto others. Security issues and self-esteem may relate to one's physical appearance. Benefit comes through working with others.

Midheaven—Can be driven to prove one's worth through one's career or societal position. May marry for emotional or financial security. Benefit comes through setting goals within the development of a positive relationship with one's self.

Moon–Mars

Moon (the emotional need) quindecile Mars (application of energy in the form of action)—May be aggressive in fulfilling one's needs and desires. Can be emotionally abusive and ruthless. Moods may change easily. Can become easily frustrated and angry. Can have strong and passionate emotional convictions. Putting these convictions into action can result in positive outcomes.
Arthur Ashe, Henry VIII, Janis Joplin

When incorporated with:

Jupiter—May have an exaggerated need to justify one's actions. Can be overly aggressive or optimistic in an attempt to meet one's needs. Can have dramatic emotional responses. Benefit can come through developing belief systems that promote a feeling of security.

Saturn—Emotional expression may be inhibited. Can become authoritative in one's actions because of emotional insecurity. Excellent for setting goals and putting them into action. Benefit comes from becoming assertive when feeling emotionally insecure.

Uranus—May be driven by an emotional need for stimulation and excitement. May take risks and "live on the edge." Can be sexually irresponsible. Can intensify temperament, and explosions may come "out of the blue." Can be beneficial when making drastic changes in one's life.

Neptune—May act on an emotional need to escape through addictions and overindulgence. Can act on intuition without hesitation. May act in a deceitful manner to get one's emotional needs met. Can be beneficial in developing spiritual concepts and understanding how to "let go and let God."

Pluto—Control, manipulation, and abuse can be prominent. May become overbearing and aggressive in an attempt to meet one's emotional needs. Can be relentless in pursuit of what one wants. Benefit can come through taking action on powerful insights and perceptions.

North Node—May push one's self into a position of renown because of insecurity. The maternal relationship may have been aggressive. Can be helpful in taking action in one's life to achieve goals and realize potentials.

Ascendant—Emotional insecurity with others can be demonstrated through aggressiveness. Obsessions are seen through what one does. Working with other people to help redirect one's focus brings benefit.

Midheaven—Self-promotion drives one's career. May marry impulsively to get ahead or to meet one's emotional needs. Benefit comes through setting goals and using this energy to achieve them.

Moon–Jupiter

Moon (the emotional need) quindecile Jupiter (excess, expansion, and growth)—May have overblown emotional reactions. Religious zeal, prejudices, and opinionation may be based on early upbringing. Indulgences can be prominent. Can be idealistic or always see the positive side of life. Can be a "Polyanna." Education is essential for positive manifestation of this aspect. Teaching abilities may be prominent. Dream big—but realistically!
Pablo Picasso, Marlene Dietrich, Brigham Young

When incorporated with:

Saturn—Emotional reactions may run "hot and cold." Grand ambitions may take center stage to obtain emotional security. Excellent when used toward positive and realistic goal setting.

Uranus—Excessive need for excitement can promote risk taking. Emotional expression can be exaggerated and unpredictable. Beneficial for changing old opinions and beliefs that come from one's early development.

Neptune—Obsession, addictions, and escapism can be prominent. Exaggerated, idealized perceptions may be a driving force. Artistic sensitivity and creative perceptions abound. Beneficial for development of one's spiritual concepts and beliefs.

Pluto—May feel empowered or disempowered through emotionally based childhood opinions and beliefs. May force one's agenda on others through a sense of being right. Benefit through transformation of emotionally based opinions and beliefs through education.

North Node—May use one's contacts to push one's self into recognition. The maternal relationship can be overemphasized. Education and development of one's philosophies and beliefs can lead to realization of one's life purpose.

Ascendant—May overreact emotionally with others. May take on too much in order to feel needed or secure. Benefit comes through understanding one's psychological issues developed in early childhood and how they impact one's interaction with others.

Midheaven—Can become overzealous within one's career because of emotional security issues. May overidentify with success. This is beneficial for long-range planning of one's security needs and educational goals.

Moon–Saturn

Moon (the emotional need) quindecile Saturn (demonstration of responsibility and authority)—Can be prone to isolation and a need for privacy because of emotional insecurity. May be driven by a fear of loss. Can exhibit strong emotional control. Security may be sought through reliability of structured goals and accomplishments. May be driven to succeed to prove one's self. Can set goals and achieve them.

Dustin Hoffman, Nicolas Copernicus, Winston Churchill

When incorporated with:

Uranus—May be driven to rebel against feelings of restriction. Intensification of self-doubt can promote an "I don't care" attitude. May take risks because of a fear of failure. Benefit comes through breaking away from childhood issues of self-doubt by setting unique and innovative goals. May become part of a cause or movement to change societal restrictions.

Neptune—May be driven to escapism or addictions because of emotional insecurity. Undefined fear of authority can drive one's life. Feelings of loss and powerlessness may be prominent. May be prone to workaholism. May avoid dealing with feelings at all costs. Benefit comes through learning to trust others and developing spiritual concepts.

Pluto—May use calculated manipulation and power to achieve one's goals. May be plagued by an obsessive fear of authority. May become overpowered by feelings of insecurity and inferiority. Benefit comes through achieving goals of self-evaluation and transformation of emotional difficulties.

North Node—Can be thrust into a position of recognition within one's career. Emotional insecurities may be present through the maternal relationship. Emotional healing for one's self and working with others toward emotional healing can become part of one's life purpose.

Ascendant—Withdrawal and controlled self-reserve may be projected through one's personality. May be driven by the emotional need for others to recognize one's achievements. May feel insecure within one's relationships. Benefit comes through working with others and developing trust.

Midheaven—May be driven by a need to structure and plan one's career to obtain a position of authority. May be prone to workaholism to prove one's self. Marriage may be used to establish emotional security or gain societal position. Beneficial when setting goals to develop self-confidence.

Moon–Uranus

Moon (the emotional need) quindecile Uranus (disruption of the status quo)—May be impulsive in taking action to fulfill one's emotional needs. Can be emotionally distant and aloof. May have a fear of attachment. May insist on doing things one's own way. May be driven to "live on the edge." May take pride in one's individuality. Can be a trendsetter. Great potential for breaking old patterns and habits.
Wilt Chamberlain, Spencer Tracy

When incorporated with:

Neptune—Erratic emotional responses and emotional upheaval can lead to escapism and addictions. Unrealistic expectations may be prominent. The need for constant excitement and stimulation can be one's escape from emotional difficulties. Benefit comes through developing one's individual spiritual concepts.

Pluto—May be driven by an intense need for freedom. Intensity of one's emotional responses may be disruptive. May feel a need to become part of societal changes. Benefit comes when making transformative changes through deep self-evaluation.

North Node—Can be thrust into renown because of one's individuality. The maternal relationship may be disruptive. This combination denotes a unique life purpose.

Ascendant—May be driven to show one's self outwardly as being unique and different. May be restless and unable to settle in one location. Benefit comes through working with others toward a common cause.

Midheaven—May be driven to express one's individuality through one's career or societal position. Can become emotionally erratic through intense focus on potential gains. Benefit through working with new societal trends and issues of independence.

Moon–Neptune

Moon (the emotional need) quindecile Neptune (seeking the illusive, imaginary, and ideal)—Addictions, fantasy, and escapism may be prominent. May get lost in one's own world. Idealism may lead to the sacrifice of one's needs. Emotional balance can be gained through spiritual insight. May be artistically sensitive and extremely creative.

Leonardo da Vinci, Lucille Ball, Ernest Hemingway

When incorporated with:

Pluto—May be driven into retreat by feelings of powerlessness. May obsess about the difficulty of life. Can be prone to escapism, addictions, or cult involvement. Insight and intuition can be prominent. Beneficial when working on intense self-evaluation with the help of a therapist, as one may not see things clearly or objectively.

North Node—May be thrust into renown through one's spiritual concepts. May pursue emotional security through others. Idealization of the maternal relationship may be prominent. Benefit comes through spiritual understanding as the life purpose.

Ascendant—May need to be recognized as sensitive and spiritual by others. May have difficulty setting boundaries with others. Use of deception may be prominent. Benefit comes through spiritual pursuits. Intuition and insight can be prominent. Artistic sensitivity may be prominent.

Midheaven—May be driven by idealistic expectations of one's career. May idealize the perception of marriage. Benefit through the use of one's intuition, insight, and sensitivity. Artistic abilities and creative self-expression can be prominent.

Moon–Pluto

Moon (the emotional need) quindecile Pluto (empowerment or disempowerment through perspectives)—May seek power and control to mask one's insecurity. Can resort to emotional blackmail and intimidation. Perspectives may be driven by early childhood conditioning. Can transform one's emotional basis and early childhood wounds by seeking to understand one's inner self. May be part of the evolution of mass consciousness.
May Sarton, Pope John Paul I, Liberace

When incorporated with:

North Node—May be thrust into renown because of one's use, or thirst for, power. The maternal influence may be powerful, controlling, or abusive. Can share powerful emotional convictions in relationships. Benefit comes through intense investigation into one's life and working with others to empower the masses.

Ascendant—May be driven to be perceived by others as powerful. May outwardly demonstrate manipulation and control of others. Benefit comes through the emotional transformation of one's personality. May express powerful emotional convictions to others.

Midheaven—May be driven to seek power and control within one's career or societal position. May seek a powerful marriage to build one's emotional security. Benefit comes through the transformation of one's emotional perceptions. Can possess the ability to express powerful personal convictions to transform societal perceptions.

Moon–North Node

Moon (the emotional need) quindecile North Node (life purpose, recognition and renown, the maternal influence)—May be thrust into a position of renown. May have a strong emotional connection to one's mother. May be driven by a need for relationships. May let one's emotional needs dictate and drive one's life path. Has ability to make positive use of contacts for one's own benefit and the benefit of others.
John F. Kennedy, Jr., Merv Griffin, Johnny Carson

When incorporated with:

Ascendant—May be obsessed with one's emotional security within relationships. May go overboard in making connections and contacts with others. The maternal influence may be seen through one's physical appearance and personality. Benefit comes through working with others toward a common cause.

Midheaven—Can be obsessed with one's professional and societal status. The maternal influence may be seen through one's career choice. Benefit comes through setting clear goals to heal childhood issues. Can possess leadership abilities.

Moon–Ascendant

Moon (the emotional need) quindecile Ascendant (the outer personality)—May be emotionally dependent upon others. May need one's feelings and emotions to be seen and acknowledged by others through relationships. Can be moody and unpredictable. Emotional conviction may be prominent in one's personality. Benefit comes through developing a strong, secure relationship with one's self.
Ralph Nader, Amy Fisher

When incorporated with:

Midheaven—Can become obsessive regarding one's career and societal position. Can be emotionally manipulative to get ahead. May focus on pleasing authority in order to get one's emotional needs met. Benefit comes through setting goals to understand how to blend one's inner and outer selves. May have the ability to express one's emotional convictions within a public role.

Moon–Midheaven

Moon (the emotional need) quindecile Midheaven (external focus through one's career and societal position)—May be driven to succeed or be recognized for one's abilities and accomplishments. Security may be related to approval from authorities. May either be extremely inhibited in public or may push to be seen in public. Can set goals and achieve ambitions if one's emotional needs are focused within one's career or meeting objectives.

Jim Jones, Howard Hughes, Napoleon I

Mercury

Mercury–Mars

Mercury (use of intelligence, mental comprehension and communication) quindecile Mars (application of energy in the form of action)—May be driven to act on one's ideas and thoughts. May force one's ideas on others through arguments or verbal abuse. Sexual innuendo may be prominent. May talk too much. Can possess the ability to speak one's mind directly and use communication abilities to present concepts assertively. May possess an extremely active mind.

Jack Nicholson, Nostradamus

When incorporated with:

Venus—Impulsive actions within relationships is highlighted. May scheme to fulfill one's material security needs. Benefit comes through sharing ideas with others. May possess strong creative and artistic expression.

Jupiter—May act impulsively on grandiose ideas. Acting on one's opinions, prejudices, and beliefs may be prominent. Benefit comes through the pursuit of education and the development of philosophies and belief systems.

Saturn—May be reluctant to share one's thoughts and ideas. Anger and depression may be prominent. May use communication to dictate one's authority. Benefit comes through strategic planning within one's ambitions and goals.

Uranus—Nervous energy and unpredictable actions may be prominent. Drive for constant stimulation may push one to shock others through one's use of communication. Sexual energy may be displayed openly through risky behavior. Benefit comes through making major changes in one's perceptions. Can possess a brilliant and innovative mind.

Neptune—May act on fantasy, idealism, and addictions. May have one's "head in the clouds" and act without restraint or forethought. May look at one's relationships through "rose-colored glasses" because of excitement and stimulation. Escapism and addiction to stimulation may be present. May possess artistic abilities. Benefit comes through the pursuit of spiritual development. Has the ability to use one's ideas for the benefit of others.

Pluto—Aggressiveness and overbearing personality can be present. May push one's own agenda through manipulation and ruthlessness. May have forceful perceptions and powerful convictions that drive one's life. Benefit comes through the pursuit of self-awareness and taking action to transform one's life. Can be a powerful influence when actively sharing ideas with others.

North Node—May become renowned for one's use of intelligence or communication. May be verbally aggressive within the maternal relationship. Actively seeking relationships may be prominent. Benefit comes through actively sharing ideas and information.

Ascendant—May be aggressive and use sexual innuendo to gain recognition from others. May actively seek relationships. May always take the lead in discussions. Benefit comes through sharing one's ideas. Can be a leader through the use of one's mind.

Midheaven—Can be aggressive and ruthless in advancing one's career. Pursuit of power and position may be prominent. May marry impulsively to gain recognition. Benefit comes through the use of ideas that can be shared with the world at large.

Mercury–Jupiter

Mercury (use of intelligence, mental comprehension, and communication) quindecile Jupiter (excess, expansion, and growth)—May have grandiose thinking. Opinionation and bias may be prominent. May be driven by one's belief systems, religious concepts, and philosophical ideology. Idealism may be prominent. Can possess an excellent ability to communicate through writing, speaking, and teaching. Continuous education is absolutely essential for positive manifestation of this aspect.

George H. Bush, Mohandas Gandhi

When incorporated with:

Venus—Idealization of relationships may be prominent. Personal opinions and views may interfere with one's relationships. May focus on gaining material security if relationships are not available. May make promises and not be able to keep them. Benefit comes through continual educational development and the sharing of information with others.

Saturn—May be driven by strategic plots and schemes to get ahead. May tend to overdo things because of a fear of not "measuring up." Workaholism can be prominent. May be focused on always being right or needing to make a point. Benefit comes through continued education to achieve one's ambitions and goals in life.

Uranus—Impulsive, erratic, and grandiose ideas may be prominent. Nervous energy may be present. May speak without thinking about the consequences. Benefit comes through the use of innovative ideas and original concepts to make changes. May be instrumental in provoking societal changes.

Neptune—Idealism, escapism, and addictions may be prominent. May live in a dreamworld. Can become obsessed with one's beliefs. Benefit comes through the continuous development of spiritual concepts. Can be artistically sensitive and extremely creative.

Pluto—May be driven to gain excessive power and control. Verbal and mental manipulation may be prominent. Powerful belief systems may take center stage in one's life. Benefit comes through continual regeneration of one's beliefs through education. Can possess a powerful ability to communicate perspectives effectively.

North Node—Renown may come through communication of one's belief systems. Writing and speaking talents may be highlighted. Benefit comes through the development of beliefs that lead to understanding one's life purpose.

Ascendant—Ideas, conversation, and mental fixations can be prominent. May interrupt and always take the lead in conversations with others. May push one's belief systems and philosophies on others. Benefit comes through sharing educational pursuits with others within a common cause.

Midheaven—May become preachy or aggressive in promotion of one's belief systems. May have grandiose ideas of who one is and what one deserves in life. Benefit comes through the use of one's verbal and mental skills. May possess an optimistic outlook that is pleasing to others. Success may be gained through the use of one's ideas, education, and ability to communicate.

Mercury–Saturn

Mercury (use of intelligence, mental comprehension, and communication) quindecile Saturn (demonstration of responsibility and authority)—May be prone to chronic depression. Workaholism may be prominent. Hesitation in speaking, stuttering, or inability to share ideas may be present. Focus on hard work. Can possess the ability to plan well and strategically set goals. May possess a good concept of reality. Use of mental abilities, ideas, and communication may be beneficial in order to attain one's ambitions and reach one's goals.

Marilyn Monroe, Pablo Picasso, Evel Knievel

When incorporated with:

Venus—Depression within one's relationships may be prominent. May be hesitant to share one's ideas because of self-worth difficulties. May strategically plan marriage or relationships. May focus on a need for material security. Benefit comes through bringing one's ideas into reality and sharing them with others.

Uranus—May be driven to upset the status quo through the use of one's ideas. May rebel against authority. Can be prone to speaking out of turn. Benefit comes through making drastic changes in the outdated patterns in one's life. Can be instrumental in advancing major societal changes.

Neptune—Sense of loss and/or depression may be prominent. Feelings of powerlessness and an inability to deal with reality may be present. Workaholism may be present. May feel overwhelmed by those in positions of authority. Benefit comes from bringing idealistic concepts into physical reality.

Pluto—Manipulation through use of strategic planning may be present. May become driven by one's ambitions, career, and thoughts of prominence. May use one's authority to push one's own agenda forward. Benefit comes through deep psychological investigation into one's life. May possess forceful and authoritative communication abilities that can bring concepts into reality.

North Node—Recognition may come through one's ambitions. The maternal relationship may influence periods of depression. Benefit comes through sharing concrete ideas with others and working toward bringing them into reality.

Ascendant—May withdraw from social interactions. May become calculating within one's relationships. May communicate with others in a cold and distant manner. Benefit comes through learning how to trust others. May possess an excellent ability to communicate complex ideas in a manner that is easily understood by others.

Midheaven—May become fearful, authoritative, or controlling within one's career. May be cold and calculating in getting ahead. May marry for prestige. May possess an ability to communicate authoritatively to the world at large.

Mercury–Uranus

Mercury (use of intelligence, mental comprehension and communication) quindecile Uranus (disruption of the status quo through unique and innovative ideas)—May be full of nervous energy and chatter incessantly. May have innovative and possibly erratic ideas. May be driven to shock others through the use of one's ideas or communication. May possess ideas that change societal concepts. Can brainstorm well. May be an individual thinker.

Karl Marx, Henry VIII, Dr. Norman Vincent Peale

When incorporated with:

Venus—Sudden or risky relationships may be prominent. May be driven to rebel against one's commitments. May be financially erratic. May shock others through the communication of one's ideas. Benefit comes through one's innovative ideas for the benefit of others. Can be extremely artistic and creative through the use of original concepts.

Neptune—Addictions and escapism may be prominent. Idealistic and unrealistic thoughts may be present. Can get lost in mental confusion. Benefit comes through individual spiritual development. Can be extremely intuitive and insightful. May have very creative and artistic concepts.

Pluto—May tend to "blow things up" in order to change them. May be unpredictable or abusive in one's communication. May be pushy when trying to get concepts across to others. May possess powerful and unconventional ideas that change society as a whole.

North Node—Recognition and renown may come through the use of one's unique ideas and concepts. The maternal relationship may be unpredictable. May rebel against the maternal influence. Benefit comes from the use of one's creative ideas that benefit humankind. Can be brilliant. Can be an innovator of thought.

Ascendant—May need to be seen as different or unique. Relationships may be unpredictable or unconventional. May shock others through one's ideas and communication. Can be unpredictable in social situations. Benefit comes through working with others toward a common cause. Can present one's original concepts and ideas with a unique style. May have the ability to stimulate others through one's thoughts and concepts.

Midheaven—May be erratic or unpredictable in pursuit or choice of one's career. May rebel against authority or society as a whole. May marry impulsively or for shock value. May be driven to be known for one's individuality. Benefit comes through sharing unique concepts that benefit humankind. Can possess a brilliant mind.

Mercury–Neptune

Mercury (use of intelligence, mental comprehension, and communication) quindecile Neptune (seeking the illusive, imaginary, and ideal)—May be driven by fantasy and illusion. May get lost in thought or be a daydreamer. Idealism can be strong. May be deceitful in one's communication. Can have difficulty expressing one's thoughts or ideas. Can have difficulty remembering or memorizing things. Can be artistically sensitive and extremely creative. Can communicate idealistic concepts effectively. Can possess great intuition and insight.

Rudolph Nureyev, Paramahansa Yogananda, Mohandas Gandhi

When incorporated with:

Venus—Idealization of one's relationships may be prominent. May be extremely codependent. May be deceitful with one's partner in financial matters. May have difficulty sharing one's ideas and thoughts in concrete terms with others. Benefit comes from sharing one's spiritual concepts. Can be artistically sensitive and creative. Insight and intuition may be strongly highlighted.

Pluto—Manipulation through the use of idealism or deceit may occur. May be driven by visions of power. May feel powerless over one's own life. Benefit comes through spiritual transformation. Can present spiritual concepts in a powerful manner. May possess insight into mass consciousness.

North Node—Renown may come through powerful ideals and spiritual perceptions. The maternal relationship may be all-consuming. May idealize perceptions of relationships. Benefit comes from sharing one's spiritual concepts. May be intuitive and insightful about others. Can possess artistic sensitivity and creative expression.

Ascendant—May be the wallflower or the butterfly at social gatherings. May merge into relationships and leave one's self behind. Addictions and escapism may be prominent. May be deceitful with others. Benefit comes through sharing one's insights and spiritual concepts. Intuition may be highlighted. Artistic sensitivity should be shared with others.

Midheaven—Workaholism may be prominent within one's idealized goals and ambitions. Addictions and escapism may be out in the open for all to see. May be unable to manifest success on a physical level. Benefit comes from sharing one's insights through one's profession or to the world at large. May possess extraordinary spiritual concepts and an ability to convey them to the world.

Mercury–Pluto

Mercury (use of intelligence, mental comprehension, and communication) quindecile Pluto (empowerment or disempowerment through perceptions)—Can be cunning, persuasive, and manipulative through the use of communication and information. May dominate and control conversations. May possess the ability to communicate powerful ideas that transform perceptions.
Paramahansa Yogananda, Mohandas Gandhi, Joan of Arc

When incorporated with:

Venus—May be driven to share one's perceptions, whether invited to or not. May plot and scheme toward financial gain or in relationships. May try to control others through communication, verbal abuse, or manipulation. Benefit comes through sharing one's perceptions with others. May possess natural psychological insight.

North Node—Renown may come through sharing one's powerful perceptions. The maternal relationship may be overpowering or empowering. Benefit comes through sharing one's perceptions. May possess perceptions that can transform others and/or the world.

Ascendant—May be manipulative or verbally abusive with others or in relationships. May push one's own agenda to the front through force of ideas. Benefit comes through sharing one's perceptions with others. Can possess the ability to communicate dynamically and powerfully.

Midheaven—Power and control issues may be focused within one's career. May use manipulation for one's benefit. May marry for power, success, or prestige. Benefit comes through setting goals to share one's perceptions. Can have the potential for major success or to make a major impact on society as a whole.

Mercury–North Node

Mercury (use of intelligence, mental comprehension, and communication) quindecile North Node (life purpose, recognition and renown, the maternal influence)—Renown may come through the use of one's ideas and intelligence. Perceptions may be driven by patterns within the maternal relationship or one may rebel against mother's ideas and perspectives. May be at ease with others because of shared perceptions and ideas. Social outreach may need a common objective. Can be social butterfly.

Doris Day, Lena Horne, Janis Joplin

When incorporated with:

Venus—Renown may come through one's relationships. The maternal relationship may influence how one deals with others. Financial matters may be prominent. Benefit comes through sharing one's ideas and perceptions with others.

Ascendant—May be driven to push one's ideas onto others. May take the lead in communication in social situations. May take on the views and perceptions of one's mother. Benefit comes through sharing one's concepts and ideas in relationships and with others.

Midheaven—Renown may come through one's career or societal position. May marry to gain recognition. The maternal relationship may influence one's choice of career. Benefit comes through sharing one's ideas and perceptions within one's career or to the world at large.

Mercury–Ascendant

Mercury (use of intelligence and communication) quindecile Ascendant (the outer personality)—May be driven toward social interaction. Can be a chatterbox. Verbal communication not tempered may result in "foot in mouth" syndrome. May put one's thoughts out for all to review. Can have a gift for public speaking and presenting ideas or concepts.
Princess Anne, George Patton

When incorporated with:

Venus—May be focused on material security or gain. May become mentally obsessed with relationships. May share too much information with others. Benefit comes through understanding and valuing who one is in relation to others.

Midheaven—May use one's ideas and intelligence to gain recognition. May be driven to be smarter, brighter, and more informed than everyone else. May use one's relationships to get ahead. Benefit comes through sharing one's ideas and thoughts in the professional arena.

Mercury–Midheaven

Mercury (use of intelligence and communication) quindecile Midheaven (external focus through one's career and societal position) —Ideas may be focused on the question "How do I get ahead?" May be driven to share one's ideas with others without any thought of the consequences. Can possess successful planning abilities and a gift for brainstorming. Receiving recognition for the use of one's ideas and communication is essential. Can be excellent at selling ideas to others.
Allen Ginsberg, Lena Horne

When incorporated with:

Venus—The need for relationships is heightened. May focus on material security if emotional security is not present. Benefit comes through self-awareness and sharing one's ideas.

Venus

Venus–Mars

Venus (the need to cooperate and collaborate) quindecile Mars (application of energy in the form of action)—May be driven toward the pursuit of relationships. Can manifest as a battle between love and war, or between being gentle or brutal. Can be the chronic flirt. May be sexually driven. Can possess artistic sensitivity and creativity in whatever one does.
Nostradamus

When incorporated with:

Jupiter—Relationship needs may be exaggerated. May become flamboyant within one's sexual desires. May be driven by a need to pursue wealth. May pursue idealistic concepts. May be overindulgent. Benefit comes through developing a relationship with one's self. May have the ability to mediate. Artistic endeavors may take on grand proportions.

Saturn—May have difficulty with relationships because of an authoritative stance. May use one's authority to gain sexual favors. The father, or authoritative parent, may influence how one interacts with one's partner. May be driven to attain material wealth through one's ambitions. Benefit comes through setting goals and taking action to reach them.

Uranus—May be driven by a need for stimulation. May be prone to rebel or disconnect from others. May take risks within sexual activity. A need for excitement may be prominent. Benefit comes through breaking old patterns in how one deals with others and developing a new, individual style of interaction.

Neptune—Codependency, addictions, and escapism may be prominent. Can be prone to idealism. Benefit comes through the development of a spiritual relationship. May have the ability to share idealistic or spiritual concepts with others.

Pluto—May become overbearing and controlling within one's relationships. May be driven toward power and financial gain. May be manipulative with others. Benefit comes through working with others in areas that require intense transformation and regeneration.

North Node—Renown may come through one's relationships. The maternal influence may impact one's current relationships. Benefit comes through sharing with others and working toward a common cause.

Ascendant—May be forceful in needing to share one's self with others. May take the lead in relationships. May become obsessed with sex or the attainment of wealth. Benefit comes through sharing with others and working toward a common cause.

Midheaven—May use one's relationships to gain social position. May seek financial gain through relationships or sexual encounters. Can become obsessed with success and social position. Benefit comes through sharing with others and working toward a common goal.

Venus–Jupiter

Venus (the need to cooperate and collaborate) quindecile Jupiter (excess, expansion, and growth)—May be excessively driven with a need for relationships and/or money. Codependency may be an issue. Morals and ethics may be based on those of one's partner and on material gain. Idealism can be present. Excess and indulgence may be prominent. Belief systems may become the major motivator, so education is essential for positive manifestation of this aspect. Can have extensive artistic and creative talents.
Fred Astaire, Merv Griffin, Carry Nation

When incorporated with:

Saturn—May have difficulty and be withdrawn in one's relationships because of an authoritative stance. May need to prove a point with the choice of one's partner. May run "hot and cold" in relationships. Material gain may be the focus of one's ambitions. Benefit comes through incorporation of education into one's goals and ambitions. Can set goals well and make great achievements.

Uranus—May be driven to erratic and unconventional relationships. The need for stimulation and excitement may be prominent. May make many changes in one's career path. May become obsessed with being unique and different. Benefit comes through making appropriate changes within one's value systems. Can be extremely creative and artistic, with a unique sense of style.

Neptune—Addictions, escapism, and codependency may be prominent. May sacrifice all for one's partner. Idealism within one's philosophies and belief systems may be present. Benefit comes through educational emphasis and the development of one's spiritual concepts. Can be artistically sensitive and very creative. Intuition and insight can be highlighted.

Pluto—May be overbearing and controlling within one's relationships. May push one's own agenda through manipulation for financial gain. Self-worth issues may be prominent. May be empowered through passionate opinions and beliefs. Benefit comes through intense psychological awareness of one's self in relation to others. May possess powerful artistic expression. The sharing of one's beliefs may lead to prominence. Can become extremely successful in life.

North Node—May be thrust into renown through one's philosophies in life. The maternal relationship may influence one's belief systems and relationships. Benefit comes through sharing one's concepts with others. Educational pursuits may be part of one's life path.

Ascendant—May push one's philosophies and belief systems onto others. May be a "know-it-all." Can be prone to weight problems.

Excess, addictions, or codependency may be prominent. Benefit comes through the development of a strong sense of self-worth. Can become successful through sharing one's concepts and opinions with others. May be extremely artistic and creative.

Midheaven—May be driven in the attainment of success and reward. May force one's opinions on others through a position of authority. May marry to gain prestige or social position. Benefit comes through continued educational development within one's career. Can be artistically successful. May become known for one's beliefs and philosophies. Major success in life is possible with this combination.

Venus–Saturn

Venus (the need to cooperate and collaborate) quindecile Saturn (the demonstration of responsibility and authority)—May use one's ambitions and goals as a substitute for relationships. Fear of intimacy, love, relationships, and loss of material gains may be prominent. May withhold sharing and suppress one's relationships. Benefit comes through setting goals of intimacy and working toward them. May be ambitious and materially successful. Needs to learn to trust in relationships and in the unknown.
Oral Roberts

When incorporated with:

Uranus—May upset the status quo and be erratic in one's relationships. May be authoritative and distant. May make changes in one's career and ambitions impulsively. May possess an intensified need to realize one's ambitions. Benefit comes through making changes in one's concepts of material success and relationships. May work with others to make major societal changes.

Neptune—Workaholism or addictions may be prominent. May assume too much responsibility for others. May have difficulty trusting others. Can have undefined fears or a fear of loss in relationships or financial areas. May idealize one's ambitions. May sacrifice everything for material gain. May be deceitful to attain one's goals. Benefit comes through setting spiritual development goals and learning to share.

Pluto—May be overbearing, controlling, and manipulative in one's relationships. May push one's own agenda through an authoritative position to ensure financial gain. May be ruthless in one's drive for success. Benefit comes through working with others in powerful and transformative ways. Can play a major role in societal shifts of consciousness.

North Node—May be thrust into renown through one's ambitions. The maternal relationship may have been distant. The maternal relationship may influence one's marital relationship. Benefit comes through the development of ambitions that are beneficial for others. With this combination, part of one's life purpose is about learning to develop trust in others.

Ascendant—May be distant and cold with others. May retreat from social situations. May take an authoritative role with others and in one's relationships. May be driven to prove one's self to others to gain self-worth. Benefit comes through working with others in a structured process that benefits everyone.

Midheaven—May be driven by one's career and ambitions. May marry for prestige and societal position. May measure one's success through material gain. Benefit comes through working toward one's ambitions, but always taking the needs of others into account within that process. Can become very successful with this combination.

Venus–Uranus

Venus (the need to cooperate and collaborate) quindecile Uranus (disruption of the status quo through unique and innovative ideas)—May be driven toward constant stimulation and excitement in one's relationships. May be sexually flirtatious and a risk taker. Can have trouble with intimacy and monogamous relationships. May be unpredictable and erratic in financial matters. Benefit comes through development of a unique sense of style and an intense focus on self-worth issues. May possess avant garde artistic talent that expresses one's own style.

Spencer Tracy, Sean Connery, David Bowie

When incorporated with:

Neptune—Addictions and escapism may be prominent. May be idealistic in one's relationships. May be unpredictable and unreliable regarding financial matters. Benefit comes through the development of individual spiritual concepts and then sharing them with others. Can possess a sensitive yet exciting artistic talent. Can be highly intuitive and insightful.

Pluto—May be driven by powerful sexual urges. May be controlling and distant within one's relationships. May manipulate others through financial instability. Benefit comes through making transformative changes in the perception of one's self-worth. Can share powerful and unique perspectives. May play a major role in societal shifts of consciousness.

North Node—May be thrust into renown through one's artistic expression or unique relationships. The maternal relationship may have been erratic and powerfully influential. Benefit comes through the development of individual style and self-assurance. Can share unique perspectives with others.

Ascendant—May be unreliable and unpredictable within one's relationships and with others in general. May use sexual flirtation as social interaction. May be driven to be seen by others as unique and different. Benefit comes through sharing one's personal and individual ideas with others. Can possess extremely creative and artistic talents and a sense of individual style.

Midheaven—May be driven by a need for excitement within one's career. May rebel against authority. May marry to shock others or to upset the status quo. May be driven to make many changes within one's career and societal position. Benefit comes through sharing one's unique ideas and concepts with the world at large. May become very successful through the use of one's unique artistic talents.

Venus–Neptune

Venus (the need to cooperate and collaborate) quindecile Neptune (seeking the illusive, imaginary, and ideal)—May be driven by illusion, idealization, and codependency in one's relationships. Fantasy, escapism, indulgences, and addictions may be prominent. Can have difficulty handling financial matters. Can possess enormous artistic sensitivity and a creative sense of style. Benefit comes through the pursuit of one's spiritual development. Can be highly intuitive and insightful with others.

Princess Diana, Brigham Young, Rudolph Nureyev

When incorporated with:

Pluto—May use manipulation to deceive others. May be domineering in one's relationships or feel abused in relationships. May use deceit and illusion to gain power and control. Benefit comes through the empowerment of spiritual concepts. Can possess powerful artistic expression. May possess spiritual perspectives to be shared with others. May play a role within the evolution of mass consciousness.

North Node—May be thrust into renown through the sensitivity of one's artistic expression. The maternal relationship may be perceived as ideal. Benefit comes through sharing one's spiritual sensitivity and artistic expression. May be intuitive and insightful with others.

Ascendant—May have difficulty setting boundaries with others. Can be prone to addictions. May play the role of victim or martyr. Can be deceitful with others. Benefit comes through the development of one's spiritual values and sharing one's sensitive artistic expression.

Midheaven—May be driven by illusion within one's career. May be deceitful in monetary matters. May have difficulty manifesting a direction in one's life. Benefit comes through the development of spiritual values. May become successful through artistic creativity.

Venus–Pluto

Venus (the need to cooperate and collaborate) quindecile Pluto (empowerment or disempowerment through perspectives)—May use manipulation and control with others. Can be driven by powerful sexual needs. Can be manipulative in financial matters. Power and money can be seen as interchangeable. Benefit comes through transformative experiences within one's relationships and the sharing of one's perspectives.

Herman Goering, Patty Hearst, Muhammad Ali

When incorporated with:

North Node—May be thrust into renown through the use or misuse of power. The maternal relationship may have been overpowering or instrumental in the development of one's personal sense of power. Benefit comes through the sharing of one's personal perspectives and an understanding of the need to share power. Sharing personal perspectives may bring one recognition or prominence.

Ascendant—May push one's own agenda onto others for financial gain. May dominate social situations. Can be controlling in one's relationships. Benefit comes through the transformation of one's values and sharing one's perspectives with others.

Midheaven—May be driven by a need for power over others within one's career and societal position. May marry for prestige and power. May be manipulative in order to get ahead. Benefit comes through the transformation of one's concepts of success. May be successful through the sharing of one's perspectives with the world at large.

Venus–North North

Venus (the need to cooperate and collaborate) quindecile North Node (the life purpose, recognition and renown, the maternal influence)—May be thrust into renown through one's artistic expression or sense of style. May be driven by values learned from one's mother. May fall in love with every new encounter. Benefit comes through learning how to share with others. Can be extremely artistic and creative. May be adept at networking and socializing.
Lena Horne, Joan Crawford, Ernest Hemingway

When incorporated with:

Ascendant—May be thrust into renown through one's relationships or artistic expression. May be influenced by one's mother in terms of physical appearance and sense of style. May be driven by a need for relationships. Benefit comes through sharing with others while maintaining one's own personal values. Can be socially appropriate at all times. May be extremely artistic and creative.

Midheaven—May be thrust into renown through one's marriage or artistic acclaim. May be influenced by one's mother regarding one's career. May be driven by ambition and monetary gain. Benefit comes through sharing one's values with others. May be very successful through one's artistic expression.

Venus–Ascendant

Venus (the need to cooperate and collaborate) quindecile Ascendant (the outer personality)—May use one's charm to get what one wants. May be driven by a desire to be beautiful. May be caught up in always having to be "nice." Can always "put one's best foot forward," but needs to focus on meeting one's own needs first and then those of others. May be artistic, creative, and have an eye for balance and design.

Marlene Dietrich, Joan Crawford, Jonathan Winters

When incorporated with:

Midheaven—May use one's charm and beauty to get ahead. May focus on financial gain within the development of one's career and ambitions. May marry for wealth or societal position. Benefit comes through sharing one's values and resources with others. Can achieve success through one's artistic expression and creativity.

Venus–Midheaven

Venus (the need to cooperate and collaborate) quindecile Midheaven (the external focus through one's career and societal position)—May use one's beauty, charm, or seduction to succeed. Money and social standing may become the goal within one's relationships. May marry the boss to get ahead. Benefit comes through sharing one's values and resources through a position of authority. Can be successful through artistic and creative means.

Princess Diana, Paul Joseph Goebbels, Lena Horne

Mars

Mars–Jupiter

Mars (application of energy in the form of action) quindecile Jupiter (excess, expansion, and growth)—May be driven by a "thirst for more." Can be extremely selfish and self-indulgent. May take on too many things at one time. One's physical energy may require an outlet to prevent outbursts of aggression, anger, or unpredictable behavior. May like to "go for the gusto." Can be excessively sexually active. May rush to judgment. Can be extremely competitive. May act impulsively on one's beliefs and opinions. Positive outreach possible through the use of one's tremendous energy directed into benefic activities like Habitat for Humanity.
H. G. Wells, Bobby Fischer

When incorporated with:

Saturn—May be forceful in trying to prove one's point. May assert too much authority over others. May be extremely ambitious. Workaholism may be prominent. Can benefit from setting educational goals in line with one's ambitions. Can become a leader in promotion of one's belief systems.

Uranus—May be driven by excessive nervous energy. May need constant stimulation and excitement. May be rebellious or argumentative. May get caught up in sexual exploits that are erratic, unpredictable, or risky. Benefit comes through learning how to assert one's individuality in an appropriate manner. Can become successful through a "stroke of luck." Needs to share one's unique and creative ideas actively with others.

Neptune—May be driven by addictions, escapism, or illusion. Can be idealistic. May become involved with cults. May use deceit to gain favor. Benefit comes through educational pursuit of one's spiritual concepts. Can be a leader in spiritual movements.

Pluto—May be excessively overbearing and controlling. May be manipulative to get what one wants. May be overly forceful and aggressive with others. Benefit comes through the transformation of one's perspectives through educational development. Can use one's amazing strength and determination to move mountains.

North Node—May be thrust into renown through the use of one's physical strength or the pursuit of one's belief systems. The maternal relationship may influence one's personal philosophies, beliefs, and self-confidence. Benefit comes through the development of one's personal philosophies and then learning how to share them with others. Can become successful simply because of an optimistic belief in what one can do.

Ascendant—May use one's physical abilities to impress others. May use sexual aggression as social interaction. May overreact with others. May be extremely overindulgent. Benefit comes through educational pursuit of one's belief systems and sharing with others. Can be very physically active and strong.

Midheaven—May be driven by a need to be successful at all costs. May marry to gain advantage. Can be aggressive and ruthless in pursuit of one's goals. Benefit comes through the development of one's belief systems and philosophies through education and awareness of others. Can be successful in whatever one attempts to do.

Mars–Saturn

Mars (application of energy in the form of action) quindecile Saturn (the demonstration of responsibility and authority)—May be driven toward one's goals, ambitions, and achievements. Can be aggressive and ruthless in pursuit of one's ambitions. May be a workaholic to prove one's self. May have a tendency to push the limits of one's physical endurance. May clash with authority. Benefit comes through setting goals that are achievable and then realizing them.
Nicole Brown Simpson, Ricki Reeves

When incorporated with:

Uranus—May be driven to rebel against authority. May make constant changes in one's career and goals. May be driven to express one's individuality and uniqueness through one's goals and ambitions. Benefit comes through setting goals that help define one's individuality. May play a role within rebellions and societal changes.

Neptune—Workaholism and other addictions may be prominent. May be idealistic in pursuit of one's ambitions. May be driven by a fear of loss. Can be deceitful in meeting one's goals and achieving one's ambitions. Benefit comes through setting spiritual goals and through the active development of one's spiritual concepts. Can make successful use of one's intuition and insight in one's career.

Pluto—May be overbearing, controlling, and manipulative in attaining one's ambitions. May be ruthless in pursuit of authority and achievement. May be driven by feelings of powerlessness and a lack of authority. Benefit comes through the transformation of one's perceptions regarding what constitutes a successful life. May play a major role through the use of one's powerful perceptions to transform societal perceptions.

North Node—May be thrust into renown through one's ambitions and realizing one's goals. The maternal relationship may have been distant and task-oriented. Benefit comes through sharing one's goals and working toward them with others. Can achieve success with this combination.

Ascendant—May be driven by ambition. May use aggression and intimidation to achieve one's goals. May be aggressive and ruthless in pursuit of relationships. May take an authoritative role with others. May take on too much responsibility for others. May push the limits of one's physical endurance. Benefit comes through sharing one's goals and working toward them with others.

Midheaven—May be driven to use aggression and intimidation within one's ambitions. May take an authoritative role in one's career. May marry impulsively to get ahead. May take on too much responsibility to prove one's self. Benefit comes through setting realistic goals and working toward them. May have ambitions that improve the reality of the world at large.

Mars–Uranus

Mars (application of energy in the form of action) quindecile Uranus (disruption of the status quo through use of unique and innovative ideas)—May be driven toward stimulation and excitement. May be irresponsible, erratic, or unpredictable in one's sexual expression. May "live on the edge" and take risks. Can have nervous energy. May shock others by actions taken. Benefit comes through breaking old habits and developing new ones.
Elvis Presley, Jimi Hendrix, Frank Sinatra

When incorporated with:

Neptune—Addictions and escapism may be prominent. May be irresponsible and deceitful. May be driven by idealistic perceptions of one's uniqueness. Benefit comes through working with one's individual spiritual development. Can possess incredible intuition and insight. Can be intensely artistic and creative.

Pluto—May manipulate and control others by keeping them on the "edge." May be obsessed with a need to be unique. Benefit comes through transforming old ways of doing things. May play a role within societal shifts and changes.

North Node—Renown may result through one's expression of individuality. The maternal relationship may have been unique, detached, or different in some way. Benefit comes through sharing one's unique perceptions with others of how to do things differently.

Ascendant—May be seen as a rebel. May have difficulty committing to relationships. May be irresponsible with others. May have a unique physical appearance. Benefit comes through working with others to make a significant societal contribution.

Midheaven—May constantly change direction in one's career. May marry impulsively. May rebel against authority. Benefit comes through the use of innovative ideas in one's career.

Mars–Neptune

Mars (the application of energy in the form of action) quindecile Neptune (seeking the illusive, imaginary, and ideal)—May use one's personal magnetism for seduction. Addictions and escapism may be prominent. May use one's sexuality in an aggressive manner. May be driven by a need to focus on the unknown, unconscious, or subconscious. Sexuality, illusion, fantasy, and deceit can be played out. Benefit comes through the pursuit of one's spiritual development. Can be artistic and creative.
Madonna, Sigmund Freud, James Van Praagh

When incorporated with:

Pluto—May be manipulative and deceitful. May use underhanded means to gain power and control. May feel powerless and overwhelmed. Benefit comes through the empowerment of one's spiritual concepts. Can be involved in transforming mass consciousness.

North Node—May be thrust into renown through one's spiritual or artistic activities. The maternal relationship may have been abusive or spiritually empowering. Benefit comes through the transformation of one's spiritual perceptions.

Ascendant—May be driven to use deceit with others. May be codependent or addicted to relationships. May be driven to be seen as artistic or sensitive. Benefit comes through sharing one's spiritual concepts. May possess insight and intuition.

Midheaven—May use deceit in one's career. May marry because of idealistic perceptions. May sacrifice one's self to get ahead. Benefit comes through setting goals of spiritual development. Can be successful through artistic expression, intuition, and insight.

Mars–Pluto

Mars (the application of energy in the form of action) quindecile Pluto (empowerment or disempowerment through perspectives) —May be driven toward power, domination, greed, and possessiveness. May demonstrate sexual dominance and aggressiveness. May be ruthless and manipulative to attain power and control. Benefit comes through the power of physical action in one's life. May use one's powerful perspectives to make societal changes.
Marie Curie, Martina Navratilova

When incorporated with:

North Node—May be thrust into renown through the power of one's perceptions. The maternal relationship may be a powerful influence in one's life. Benefit comes through sharing one's perspectives with others. This combination can bring success in whatever one desires. Transforming societal perceptions may be one's life purpose.

Ascendant—May use force or ruthless manipulation with others. May be obsessed with relationships. May use one's physical strength and determination to define one's self. Benefit comes through sharing one's powerful perceptions with others.

Midheaven—May be ruthless and aggressive in pursuit of one's career and societal position. May marry for prestige or social position. May dominate and control others in an attempt to reach one's ambitions. Benefit comes through the use of one's powerful perceptions within one's career. Can play a role transforming perceptions of the world at large.

Mars–North Node

Mars (the application of energy in the form of action) quindecile North Node (the life purpose, recognition and renown, the maternal influence)—May be aggressive and angry with others. May be abusive in one's relationships. May be driven by resentment and anger within the maternal relationship. May have been taught assertiveness through the maternal influence. Benefit comes through learning the difference between assertiveness and aggressiveness. May become known for use of one's physical energy.

When incorporated with:

Ascendant—May be aggressive in one's relationships with others. May react and respond by copying one's mother's reactions. Benefit comes through working with others toward a common goal. May be thrust into recognition or renown through what one does in life.

Midheaven—May be aggressive in one's career. May marry impulsively to gain societal position. May react aggressively with those in authority or push to take an authority role. Benefit comes through working with others to achieve a common goal. May become known for one's physical applications in life.

Mars–Ascendant

Mars (the application of energy in the form of action) quindecile Ascendant (the outer personality)—Aggressiveness, anger, and resentment may be prominent. May be aggressive within one's relationships. May have the ability to assert one's self physically to get what one wants. May use one's physical energy to identify one's self. May work hard for the benefit of others.
Oral Roberts, Albert Einstein, Prince Andrew

When incorporated with:

Midheaven—May be aggressive in obtaining goals within one's career. May marry impulsively to gain advantage. Benefit comes through understanding the difference between being aggressive and being assertive. May become known for one's physical strength, attributes, or appearance.

Mars–Midheaven

Mars (the application of energy in the form of action) quindecile Midheaven (external focus through one's career and societal position)—May be aggressive or ruthless in one's career and goal setting. May step on others to get ahead. May be driven by a need to reach the top. May marry to gain societal position. Benefit comes through the assertive pursuit of one's goals. Can demonstrate confidence when doing what one is passionate about.

Paul Newman, Oprah Winfrey

JUPITER

Jupiter–Saturn

Jupiter (excess, expansion, and growth) quindecile Saturn (the demonstration of responsibility and authority)—May be indecisive or run "hot and cold." May push to make one's point. May overdo things and assume excess responsibility to gain approval. May take an authoritative position in one's beliefs and opinions. May seek reward for one's efforts. May retreat within one's success. Benefit comes through the use of ethics and morals. Can have the ability to evaluate opportunities and plan successfully.

Jackie Kennedy Onassis, Clint Eastwood, Princess Anne

When incorporated with:

Uranus—May be driven to rebel against law and order. May disrupt the status quo to make a point. Benefit comes through using one's innovative ideas to make positive societal changes.

Neptune—May be driven by idealism in one's career. May lose one's self in one's work. Benefit comes through defining one's spiritual beliefs.

Pluto—May be manipulative, controlling, and overbearing in one's ambitions. May demonstrate authority through one's opinions. Benefit comes through the transformation of societal perceptions, philosophies, and belief systems.

North Node—May be thrust into renown through one's accomplishments. The maternal relationship may influence one's beliefs. Benefit comes through working with others toward common objectives.

Ascendant—May run "hot and cold." May assume excess responsibility in order to prove one's self. Benefit comes through becoming an authority within one's own belief systems.

Midheaven—May be driven by grandiose dreams of success. May marry to gain advantage. May use excessive authority to gain recognition. Benefit comes through realistic goal setting that incorporates one's beliefs and philosophies.

Jupiter–Uranus

Jupiter (excess, expansion, and growth) quindecile Uranus (disruption of the status quo through unique and innovative ideas)—May be driven to "push the envelope." Can be a risk taker. May possess an addiction to excitement and stimulation. May rebel against common belief systems and philosophies to promote one's individuality. Benefit comes through seeking innovative ways to benefit humankind and promote equality for all. Can break new ground, especially in the advancement of new technologies, ideas, and concepts.
Dave Brubeck, H. G. Wells, Linda Lovelace

When incorporated with:

Neptune—Addictions, confusion, and escapism may be prominent. May rebel because of one's idealistic beliefs. Benefit comes through developing individual spiritual beliefs. Can be influential in expanding societal spiritual perceptions.

Pluto—May manipulate and control by catching others "off guard." May be driven to take chances and risks. Benefit comes through disrupting old belief systems through innovative perspectives. May influence changes in mass consciousness.

North Node—May be thrust into renown through one's rebelliousness or unique style. Benefit comes through the sharing of one's innovative concepts, philosophies, and beliefs with others.

Ascendant—May be driven to be different and unique. May shock others through one's physical appearance. Benefit comes through the sharing of one's unique philosophies and beliefs.

Midheaven—May make continuous changes in one's career. May marry impulsively to disrupt the status quo. Benefit comes through sharing one's unique philosophies and beliefs.

Jupiter–Neptune

Jupiter (excess, expansion, and growth) quindecile Neptune (seeking the illusive, imaginary, and ideal)—May be driven by indulgences, addictions, escapism, and idealism. May use illusion or deceit to gain advantage. May be continuously dissatisfied because of a dream of the ideal. Benefit comes through the pursuit of one's spiritual philosophies and beliefs. May be artistically sensitive and creative. *Mata Hari, Mark Twain, Sydney Biddle Barrow*

When incorporated with:

Pluto—May use the promise of the ideal to manipulate and control others. May become empowered or powerless through one's spiritual beliefs. Benefit comes through the intense evaluation and transformation of one's spiritual concepts. Can play a role in uplifting the mass consciousness. Powerful perspectives come through one's artistic sensitivity.

North Node—May be thrust into renown through one's spiritual concepts or the use of deceit and illusion. The maternal influence may be an illusion of the ideal. Benefit comes through sharing one's spiritual concepts and beliefs with others. May become prominent through one's use of intuition, insight, and artistic sensitivity.

Ascendant—May use deceit or illusion with others. May sacrifice one's self within relationships. May seek the ideal physical appearance. Benefit comes through sharing one's spiritual concepts and beliefs with others.

Midheaven—May be driven by visions of reward and success within one's career. May use deceit to gain advantage. Benefit comes through sharing one's spiritual beliefs within the professional arena. Can be highly intuitive, insightful, and artistic.

Jupiter–Pluto

Jupiter (excess, expansion, and growth) quindecile Pluto (empowerment or disempowerment through perspectives)—May be driven by a need for power and success. May be overly manipulative, controlling, or ruthless to gain advantage. May use one's belief systems, opinions, or religion to manipulate others. Benefit comes from transformation through internal investigation of one's belief systems. Can be a player within major societal changes and transformation of mass consciousness and perspectives.
May Sarton, Drew Barrymore

When incorporated with:

North Node—May be thrust into prominence through the power of one's philosophies, beliefs, and perspectives. The maternal relationship may have been controlling and abusive. The maternal relationship may have been influential in developing one's personal perspectives and beliefs. Benefit comes through internal investigation of one's belief systems. Can be involved with societal shifts of consciousness.

Ascendant—May use excessive manipulation with others or in one's relationships. Benefit may come through internal investigation of one's belief systems and sharing one's perspectives with others.

Midheaven—May be driven toward success and power within one's career. May marry for prestige or powerful social position. May use ruthless manipulation and control within one's career. Benefit comes through the use of transformative perceptions within one's career. May play a role in societal shifts of mass consciousness. Can become extremely successful with this combination.

Jupiter–North Node

Jupiter (excess, expansion, and growth) quindecile North Node (the life purpose, recognition and renown, the maternal influence) —May gain recognition and renown through one's philosophies and belief systems. The maternal influence may be tied into one's belief systems. May be driven to gain advantage from one's contacts and relationships with others. May be driven to push one's opinions, beliefs, and judgments on others. Benefit comes through continual education and development of one's concepts and beliefs. May work with others for the greater good.

Betty Ford, Barbara Bush, Camilla Parker Bowles

When incorporated with:

Ascendant—Recognition and renown may come through sharing one's beliefs and concepts. May mimic maternal concepts and beliefs instead of forming one's own set of beliefs. May be driven to gain advantage from one's relationships with others. May push one's opinions, beliefs, and judgments on others. Benefit comes through sharing one's concepts and beliefs with others. Can be very generous with others.

Midheaven—May gain recognition and renown through one's philosophies and belief systems. Maternal beliefs may be connected to one's career choice. May marry to gain advantage or societal position. May push one's opinions, beliefs, and judgments through one's career. Benefit comes through sharing one's concepts and beliefs within the professional arena. May become known for one's benefic works.

Jupiter–Ascendant

Jupiter (excess, expansion, and growth) quindecile Ascendant (the outer personality)—May be prone to addictions, escapism, and codependency. Excesses and indulgences may be shown through one's physical body. May push one's opinions, judgments, and beliefs on others. May take on too much. Benefit comes through sharing one's beliefs with others. Can be very optimistic and warm-hearted. Can become known internationally.

Rex Harrison, Marilyn Monroe, Nancy Kerrigan

When incorporated with:

Midheaven—May gain renown through one's philosophies and belief systems. May marry to gain advantage within one's societal position. May push one's opinions, beliefs, and judgments through one's career. May push one's self physically within one's career. Benefit comes through sharing one's concepts and beliefs within the professional arena. May work for the benefit of others. Can be very successful with this combination.

Jupiter–Midheaven

Jupiter (excess, expansion, and growth) quindecile Midheaven (the external focus through one's career and societal position)—May be driven by a need for success and recognition. May marry for status, recognition, or reward. May promote one's opinions, judgments, and beliefs through one's career or societal position. May believe that success and recognition are everything. Benefit comes through sharing one's philosophies and beliefs in the professional arena. Can be a leader for good or bad. Benefit comes through one's optimistic outlook and outreach. Can attain major success and recognition with this combination.

Barbra Streisand, Catherine the Great, Marla Maples

Author's Note

The following planetary combinations are referenced through possible societal impact instead of personal impact. These planets travel slowly within our solar system, and therefore millions of individuals are born with these same planetary combinations.

The time periods when these planetary combinations come into alignment appear to be indications of societal structure, revolution, spiritual concerns, and societal shifts in consciousness.

SATURN

Saturn–Uranus

Saturn (the demonstration of responsibility and authority) quindecile Uranus (disruption of the status quo)—May be driven toward breaking old and outdated concepts through the use of innovative ideas. May disrupt governing systems. May break the rules through defiance of law and order. Benefit comes through making societal changes for the betterment of humankind.

When incorporated with:

Neptune—Idealism pushes revolution against authority. Compassion influences disruption of societally accepted parameters. Innovative ideas permeate old systems. Deception breaks down leadership.

Pluto—Powerful perceptions stimulate revolt against authority. Innovative ideas disrupt old systems. Empowerment breaks down authoritarian control.

North Node—Can be thrust into renown by disrupting old systems. May rebel against maternal authority. Can play a role in the changing of societal systems.

Ascendant—May be driven to share revolutionary ideas with others to break down old structures. May push against the norms of society through one's personal appearance.

Midheaven—May be instrumental in changing societal systems through one's leadership. May clash with authority through one's career or societal position.

Saturn–Neptune

Saturn (the demonstration of responsibility and authority) quindecile Neptune (seeking the illusive, imaginary, and ideal)—Deception may be present within societal leadership. Rigid structure may disappear. Idealism may dissolve old systems. Compassion may merge with authority. Dreams may become reality.

When incorporated with:

Pluto—Powerful perspectives of idealism may dissolve governments. Empowerment and compassion can influence societal leadership. Deceit within authority may lead to disempowerment.

North Node—May be thrust into renown through one's idealistic perceptions. The maternal relationship may have been powerfully influential. Can play a role within societal leadership through one's compassion and idealism.

Ascendant—May be able to bring one's dreams into reality with the assistance of others. May deceive others through authoritative posturing. May show compassion to others in concrete ways.

Midheaven—May attain a position of authoritative leadership through one's sensitivity, compassion, and idealism. May deceive those in a position of authority. Can become a primary force for unity within societal leadership.

Saturn–Pluto

Saturn (the demonstration of responsibility and authority) quindecile Pluto (empowerment or disempowerment through perspectives)—Old systems may be driven toward self-destruction. Societal leaders may use force, manipulation, and control. Rigid structures may regenerate and transform. Authority may be influenced by mass consciousness.

When incorporated with:

North Node—May be thrust into renown through one's powerful perspectives within societal leadership. The maternal influence may have been strongly authoritarian or empowering. Can become part of the transformation and regeneration of old societal systems.

Ascendant—May use force, manipulation, and control with others. May "dress for success." May share one's perceptions with others, which influence societal leadership.

Midheaven—May use manipulation, control, and force within an authoritative position. May marry for powerful societal position. Can be instrumental in empowering societal leadership.

Saturn–North Node

Saturn (the demonstration of responsibility and authority) quindecile North Node (the life purpose, recognition and renown, the maternal influence)—May be thrust into renown because of one's authoritative position. The maternal influence may have been one's strongest authority. May share one's ambitions and goals with others.

When incorporated with:

Ascendant—May be a wallflower at social functions. May use one's authority to intimidate others. May dress conservatively to impress others. May share responsibility and authority with others.

Midheaven—May take on a role of responsibility and authority. May marry for societal position. May be cold and calculating to reach the top. May be a leader within societal structures through an authoritative role.

Saturn–Ascendant

Saturn (demonstration of responsibility and authority) quindecile Ascendant (the outer personality)—May hold a position of authority with others. May be driven by a need to be seen as respectable, dependable, and authoritative. Fear of sharing with others may hold one back. May measure one's self through everyone else. May have the ability to demonstrate how to set and reach goals to others.

Queen Elizabeth I, Pope John Paul I, Jimi Hendrix

When incorporated with:

Midheaven—May use one's ambitions and goals to be in a position of leadership and authority. May marry someone in a position of authority for social position. May be cold and calculating in one's "climb to the top." May play a strong role within societal leadership.

Saturn–Midheaven

Saturn (demonstration of hard work, responsibility, and ambition) quindecile Midheaven (external focus through one's career and societal position)—May be driven by a need for approval from an authoritative parent. May become one's own authority in life. May have a fear of authority. May hold one's self back in one's career. May be driven to succeed. May "climb to the top" one step at a time, but can get there.

Madonna, Nostradamus, Marilyn Monroe

URANUS

Uranus–Neptune

Uranus (disruption of the status quo through unique and revolutionary ideas) quindecile Neptune (seeking the illusive, imaginary, and ideal)—Idealism may influence rebellion. Disruption of the ideal. Disruption of unity. Deceit may disrupt the status quo. Can be a time of heightened idealism, artistic expression, and new thought. Unification through innovative ideas. Intuition and insight into the unknown. Compassion and sensitivity through honoring one's individuality.

When incorporated with:

Pluto—Powerful perceptions of idealism may upset the status quo. Rebellious unification can lead to empowerment. Mass consciousness may shift through intuition, compassion, and sensitivity. Disruption of the ideal through disempowerment, control, and manipulation.

North Node—May be thrust into renown through one's innovative and idealistic concepts. The maternal influence may have been intensely idealized. Can be a part of sharing a unifying process through revolution.

Ascendant—May be torn between merging one's self with others and showing one's individuality. May attract others through a shared vision. May be intensely idealistic in one's relationships. Can be involved in societal shifts of consciousness.

Midheaven—May be extremely artistically sensitive, creative, and innovative within one's career. May shock others through deceit. May play a role in societal shifts of consciousness through a position of leadership.

Uranus–Pluto

Uranus (disruption of the status quo through unique and innovative ideas) quindecile Pluto (empowerment or disempowerment through perceptions)—Empowerment of perspectives leads to revolution. Powerful shifts and individuality within mass consciousness. Manipulation, control, and ruthlessness used to upset the status quo. Individuality and differentiation through powerful transformation. Powerful urge for freedom. Societal reform through rebellion. Advancement through technological awareness.

When incorporated with:

North Node—One may be thrust into renown through one's unique perspectives and rebellious attitude. The maternal influence may have empowered one's individuality or overpowered one's individuality. May be part of societal shifts in consciousness.

Ascendant—May share powerful transformative perceptions and innovative ideas with others. May be forceful and unpredictable in one's relationships. May become involved in societal movements of rebellion. May have a unique and powerful sense of style.

Midheaven—May use innovative and powerful perspectives within one's career. May marry impulsively for power and societal position. May be influential in making powerful changes in society's perspectives. May play a leadership role in societal shifts of consciousness.

Uranus–North Node

Uranus (disruption of the status quo through innovative ideas) quindecile North Node (life purpose, recognition and renown, life purpose)—May become renowned for one's individuality and innovative ideas. May rebel against the maternal influence, or the maternal influence may have been unstable. May become involved in sudden and risky relationships. May be driven by a need to shock others.

Can get a different perspective on things by going outside of one's own circle.

When incorporated with:

Ascendant—May be thrust into prominence through the sharing of innovative ideas with others. May be unpredictable in one's relationships. The maternal relationship may have influenced one's individuality or may have been erratic. May become involved in societal movements of rebellion. May have a unique and powerful sense of style.

Midheaven—May use innovative ideas, technology, or creative talents within one's career. May marry impulsively. May be influential in making powerful changes within society. May play a leadership role in societal shifts of consciousness.

Uranus–Ascendant

Uranus (disrupting the status quo through unique ideas) quindecile Ascendant (the outer personality)—May identify one's self through one's individual style or personal expression. May share innovative thoughts and ideas with others. May be unpredictable within one's relationships. May become involved in sudden and risky relationships. May be driven by a need to shock others. May be part of a societal shift in technological consciousness.
Harry Houdini, George H. Bush

When incorporated with:

Ascendant—May be thrust into prominence through the sharing of innovative ideas with others. May be unpredictable in one's relationships. The maternal relationship may have influenced one's individuality or may have been erratic. May become involved in societal movements of rebellion. May have a unique and powerful sense of style.

Midheaven—May use innovative ideas, technology, or creative talents within one's career. May marry impulsively. May be influential in making powerful changes in society. May play a leadership role in societal shifts of consciousness.

Uranus–Midheaven

Uranus (disruption of the status quo through use of innovative ideas) quindecile Midheaven (external focus through one's career and societal position)—May be driven to take risks in one's career or switch jobs/career often. May be a leading force or in a position of authority within societal rebellions. Innovative ideas may be utilized within one's career or societal position. Technology or advancement of thought may be highlighted within one's career. The inventor.

David Bowie, Emmaline Pankhurst, Nicolas Copernicus

NEPTUNE

Neptune–Pluto

Neptune (seeking the illusive, imaginary, and ideal) quindecile Pluto (empowerment or disempowerment through perspectives) —Unification can lead to empowerment. Powerful perspectives of idealism. Transformation through insight. Mass consciousness may shift through intuition, compassion, and sensitivity. Manipulation and control through deception. The power of illusion.

When incorporated with:

North Node—May be thrust into renown through the use of powerful illusion or deception with others. The maternal relationship may have been manipulative and illusive. May play a role in the uplifting of mass consciousness. Can become involved in idealistic movements.

Ascendant—May feel overpowered by others. May be extremely insightful with others. May be codependent within one's relationships. May play a part in working with others to raise conscious awareness.

Midheaven—May use power, manipulation, and deceit within one's career. May marry for power. May focus one's goals in life through idealistic perceptions of transforming mass consciousness.

Neptune–North Node

Neptune (seeking the illusive, imaginary, and ideal) quindecile North Node (the life purpose, recognition and renown, the maternal relationship)—May be thrust into renown because of one's artistic sensitivity or idealism. May have idealized perceptions of one's mother. The maternal relationship may have been deceitful. May become involved with others on a "spiritual quest." May be intuitive and insightful with others. May deceive others. May play a role in the spiritual uplifting of others.

When incorporated with:

Ascendant—May have difficulty setting boundaries with others. May be codependent in one's relationships. May use illusion or deceit with others. May be intuitive and insightful with others. May become involved with others who are on a spiritual quest.

Midheaven—May be deceitful within one's career. May use intuition, insight, or artistic sensitivity within one's career. May marry the "ideal" partner. The maternal influence may be seen within one's career. May be a leading force within spiritual arenas. May play a role in the spiritual uplifting of the times.

Neptune–Ascendant

Neptune (seeking the illusive, imaginary, and ideal) quindecile Ascendant (the outer personality)—May be driven to use subterfuge or deceit with others. May be codependent or disillusioned in one's relationships. May be the eternal martyr or victim. May not be able to set boundaries with others. May be artistically sensitive. May play a role in the spiritual uplifting of the times. Spiritual sharing and artistic outreach
Eva Braun

When incorporated with:

Midheaven—May use subterfuge and deceit within one's career. May marry because one finds the "ideal" partner. May be artistically sensitive within one's career. May play a role in the spiritual uplifting of the times.

Neptune–Midheaven

Neptune (seeking the illusive, imaginary, and ideal) quindecile Midheaven (external focus through one's career and societal position)—May use illusion or deception within one's career. May have idealized perceptions about who one is in the world. May be very intuitive, insightful, or artistically sensitive within one's career. May marry because one has found the "ideal" partner. May play a role or be a leader in spiritual arenas.

Bobby Fischer, Gregory Peck, Mark Twain

PLUTO

Pluto–North Node

Pluto (empowerment or disempowerment through perspectives) quindecile North Node (the life purpose, recognition and renown, the maternal influence)—May be thrust into renown through one's powerful perspectives. May be manipulative and controlling with others. The maternal influence may have been dominant. May always connect with powerful people. May play a role in sharing perspectives that either empower or distemper others.
Fred Astaire, Heinrich Himmler, Shirley MacLaine

When incorporated with:

Ascendant—May be controlling or manipulative with others. May share transformative or empowering perspectives with others. May intimidate others through one's physical appearance. May mimic the maternal influence through one's physical appearance.

Midheaven—May be driven for power within one's career. May use manipulation or control within one's career or societal position. The maternal influence may be seen within one's career choice. May use one's societal position toward reform.

Pluto–Ascendant

Pluto (empowerment or disempowerment through perspectives) quindecile Ascendant (the outer personality)—May be forceful, manipulative, or controlling with others. May use powerful perspectives in an attempt to gain control of others. May be influential in shaping other people's perspectives. May become a leader of the masses.
Jim Jones, Sean Connery

When incorporated with:

Midheaven—May be driven by a need for power within one's career. May use one's influence over others to gain advantage in one's career and societal position. May use manipulation, control, or force within one's societal position. May become a driving force for transformation and reform of societal perceptions. May become a leader of mass movements.

Pluto–Midheaven

Pluto (empowerment and disempowerment through perceptions) quindecile Midheaven (external focus through one's career and societal position)—May be driven by a need for ultimate power within one's career. May use one's influence over others to gain advantage in one's career and societal position. May marry for a position of power within society. May become a driving force for transformation and reform of societal perceptions. May become a leader of mass movements.
Allen Ginsberg

NORTH NODE

North Node–Ascendant

North Node (the life purpose, recognition and renown, the maternal influence) quindecile Ascendant (the outer personality)—May be thrust into renown through what others think or see about one's self. The maternal influence may be seen in one's physical appearance or personal style. May share one's self with others openly. May have a major impact on others

Dr. Norman Vincent Peale, Drew Barrymore

When incorporated with:

Midheaven—May use the sharing of one's self in one's career. May use others to get ahead. May see the maternal influence within one's choice of career. May be driven to succeed. May feel driven to share everything with others.

North Node–Midheaven

North Node (the life purpose, recognition and renown, the maternal influence) quindecile Midheaven (external focus through one's career and societal position)—May push to be recognized. May use the sharing of one's self in one's career. May use others to get ahead. The maternal influence may be seen through one's choice of career. May be driven to succeed. May feel driven to share everything with others.

Jim Jones, Franklin D. Roosevelt, Howard Cosell

Bibliography

Books

American Psychiatric Association. *DSM-III-R (Diagnostic and Statistical Manual of Mental Disorders.* Washington, D.C.: American Psychiatric Association, 1987.

Andrews, Nigel. *True Myths: The Life and Times of Arnold Schwarzenegger.* New York, N.Y.: Carol Publishing Group, 1996.

de Toledano, Ralph. *Hit & Run: The Rise—and Fall?—of Ralph Nader.* New Rochelle, N.Y.: Arlington House, 1975.

Echols, Alice. *Scars of Sweet Paradise: The Life and Times of Janis Joplin.* New York, N.Y.: Henry Holt, 1999.

Edwards, Henry, and Tony Zanetta. *Stardust: The David Bowie Story.* New York, N.Y.: McGraw-Hill, 1986.

Ford, Betty. *The Times of My Life.* New York, N.Y.: Harper & Row, 1978.

Guthrie, Lee. *Woody Allen: A Biography.* New York, N.Y.: Drake Publishers, 1978.

Hogg, Ian V. *The Biography of General George S. Patton.* New York, N.Y.: Galley Press, 1982.

Leigh, Wendy. *Arnold: An Unauthorized Biography*. Chicago, Ill.: Congdon & Weed, Inc., 1990.

————. *Prince Charming: The John F. Kennedy Jr. Story*. Research by Stephen Karten. New York, N.Y.: Dutton, 1993.

Remnick, David. *King of the World: Muhammad Ali and the Rise of an American Hero*. New York, N.Y.: Random House, 1998.

Tremlett, George. *David Bowie: Living on the Brink*. New York, N.Y.: Carroll & Graf, 1996.

Tyl, Noel. *Astrology of the Famed*. St. Paul, Minn.: Llewellyn Publications, 1996.

Internet Websites

David Bowie
http://mrshowbiz.go.com/people/davidbowie/index.html
http://www.rollingstone.com/

George S. Patton
http://www.biography.com/

Jackie Robinson
White, Jack E. "Stepping Up to the Plate: Outspoken Jackie Robinson Played the Role of Symbol as Well as He Hit a Ball." *Time Magazine* 149, no. 13 (March 31, 1997).
http://www.time.com/time/magazine/1997/dom/970331/essay.steping_up_to.html

John Lennon
http://mrshowbiz.go.com/people/johnlennon/index.html
http://www.biography.com/
http://www.rollingstone.com/

Louis Pasteur
Website for the Canadian French Embassy.
http://ambafrance-ca.org/hyperlab/

Mohandas Gandhi
Gandhi: Living in Peace
http://gandhi.virtualave.net/
Website created, designed, and maintained by Leigh Angela.

Manas: History and Politics, Gandhi
http://www.sscnet.ucla.edu/southasia/History/Gandhi/gandhi.html
© (text) Vinay Lal, Assistant Professor of History, UCLA.

Dr. Norman Vincent Peale
http://www.biography.com/

Oprah Winfrey
http://mrshowbiz.go.com/people/oprahwinfrey/index.html
http://www.biography.com/

Sigmund Freud
Library of Congress Exhibitions website.
"Freud: Section One: Formative Years."
http://lcweb.loc.gov/exhibits/freud/freud01.html.

The Freud Page
http://www.geocities.com/Eureka/Promenade/1919/freudbiography.html
Website built and maintained by Maria Helena Rowell.

Index

☽ REACH FOR THE MOON

Llewellyn publishes hundreds of books on your favorite subjects! To get these exciting books, including the ones on the following pages, check your local bookstore or order them directly from Llewellyn.

ORDER BY PHONE

- Call toll-free within the U.S. and Canada, 1-800-THE MOON
- In Minnesota, call (651) 291-1970
- We accept VISA, MasterCard, and American Express

ORDER BY MAIL

- Send the full price of your order (MN residents add 7% sales tax) in U.S. funds, plus postage & handling to:

  Llewellyn Worldwide
  P.O. Box 64383, Dept. 1-56718-562-2
  St. Paul, MN 55164–0383, U.S.A.

POSTAGE & HANDLING

(For the U.S., Canada, and Mexico)

- $4.00 for orders $15.00 and under
- $5.00 for orders over $15.00
- No charge for orders over $100.00

We ship UPS in the continental United States. We ship standard mail to P.O. boxes. Orders shipped to Alaska, Hawaii, The Virgin Islands, and Puerto Rico are sent first-class mail. Orders shipped to Canada and Mexico are sent surface mail.

International orders: Airmail—add freight equal to price of each book to the total price of order, plus $5.00 for each non-book item (audio tapes, etc.).

Surface mail—Add $1.00 per item.

Allow 2 weeks for delivery on all orders.
Postage and handling rates subject to change.

DISCOUNTS

We offer a 20% discount to group leaders or agents. You must order a minimum of 5 copies of the same book to get our special quantity price.

FREE CATALOG

Get a free copy of our color catalog, *New Worlds of Mind and Spirit*. Subscribe for just $10.00 in the United States and Canada ($30.00 overseas, airmail). Many bookstores carry *New Worlds*—ask for it!

Visit our website at www.llewellyn.com for more information.

The Creative Astrologer
Effective Single-Session Counseling

Noel Tyl

The Creative Astrologer is a new point of departure for astrology: the realm of counseling effectiveness in a single-session format. For more than thirty years, renowned astrologer Noel Tyl has brought psychological methodology into astrological symbolism and analysis. Now he crowns that effort with a master volume emphasizing the techniques of counseling as part of modern astrological practice.

Tyl offers more than 700 creative connections to guide astrologers throughout planetary and aspect symbolisms into deep analysis of the human condition. He clearly develops the art of questioning, techniques for inviting disclosure, and specific objectification therapies. Every analytical insight comes from his own long career of experience, theorization, and experimentation. Verbatim examples from his own recent client sessions are used to illustrate his techniques.

1-56718-740-4, 264 pp., 7½ x 9⅛   **$17.95**

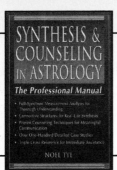

Synthesis & Counseling In Astrology
The Professional Manual

Noel Tyl

One of the keys to a vital, comprehensive astrology is the art of synthesis, the capacity to take the parts of our knowledge and combine them into a coherent whole. Many times, the parts may be contradictory (the relationship between Mars and Saturn, for example), but the art of synthesis manages the unification of opposites. Now Noel Tyl presents ways astrological measurements—through creative synthesis—can be used to effectively counsel individuals. Discussion of these complex topics is grounded in concrete examples and in-depth analyses of the 122 horoscopes of celebrities, politicians, and private clients.

Tyl's objective in providing this vitally important material was to present everything he has learned and practiced over his distinguished career to provide a useful source to astrologers. He has succeeded in creating a landmark text destined to become a classic reference for professional astrologers.

1-56718-734-X, 924 pp., 7 x 10, 115 charts   **$29.95**

Astrology
Understanding the Birth Chart

Kevin Burk

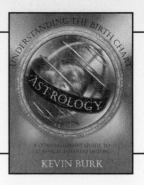

This beginning- to intermediate-level astrology book is based on a course taught to prepare students for the NCGR Level I Astrological Certification exam. It is a unique book for several reasons. First, rather than being an astrological phrase book or "cookbook," it helps students to understand the language of astrology. From the beginning, students are encouraged to focus on the concepts, not the keywords. Next, as soon as you are familiar with the fundamental elements of astrology, the focus shifts to learning how to work with these basics to form a coherent, synthesized interpretation of a birth chart. In addition, it explains how to work with traditional astrological techniques, most notably the essential dignities. All interpretive factors are brought together in the context of a full interpretation of the charts of Sylvester Stallone, Meryl Streep, Eva Peron, and Woody Allen. This book fits the niche between cookbook astrology books and more technical manuals.

- Discover how classical astrology can enrich your understanding of the planets, signs, and houses
- Use the essential dignities to determine the relative strength or weakness of a planet in a particular sign
- Explore the methodology behind the different systems of house division
- Discover the mechanics and the effects of the Moon's nodes
- Study aspect patterns and their effects in the chart
- Use the comprehensive worksheet to lead you through all the interpretive factors necessary

1-56718-088-4, 384 pp., 7½ x 9⅛, illus.   **$17.95**

A Handbook for Parents

Astrology & Your Child
A Handbook for Parents

Gloria Star

(formerly titled *Optimum Child*)
Many who face the challenges of parenthood have wished for a handbook on each child. Well, that handbook exists. It is the astrological chart! The horoscope symbolically indicates a child's physical, mental, emotional, and spiritual needs. It is an excellent tool for allowing children to be who they really are, and for helping them to develop their fullest potential. *Astrology & Your Child* is written for parents new to astrology, as well as experienced astrologers.

Since a child's expression of the Self is not yet mature, the astrological symbols must be interpreted with this in mind. Just as psychologists have put forth theories dealing specifically with the behavior and developmental stages of children, astrologers must also redefine their usual adult focus with dealing with children.

A brief table of where the planets were when your children were born is included in the book so that even if you don't have their individual birthcharts, you can find out enough to begin to help them develop their potential.

1-56718-649-1, 312 pp., 7½ x 9⅛, 84 charts   **$17.95**

Astrology for Women
Roles & Relationships

Gloria Star, editor

Despite the far-reaching alterations women have experienced collectively, individual women are still faced with the challenge of becoming themselves. In today's world, a woman's role is not defined so much by society's expectations as by the woman herself. This book is a first look at some of the tasks each woman must embrace or overcome.

Ten female astrologers explore the many facets of the soulful process of becoming a whole person:

- Jan Spiller—The Total Woman
- Demetra George—Women's Evolving Needs: The Moon and the Blood Mysteries
- M. Kelley Hunter—The Mother-Daughter Bond
- Carol Garlick—Daughter's and Fathers: The Father's Role in the Development of the Whole Woman
- Barbara Schermer—Psyche's Task: A Path of Initiation for Women
- Glória G. Star—Creating Healthy Relationships
- Madalyn Hillis-Dineen—On Singleness: Choosing to Be Me
- Ronnie Gale Dreyer—The Impact of Self-Esteem
- Kim Rogers-Gallagher—Who Should I Be When I Grow Up?
- Roxana Muise—The Sacred Sisterhood

1-56718-860-5, 416 pp., 5 ³⁄₁₆ x 8, charts   **$9.95**

To order, call 1-800-THE MOON
Prices subject to change without notice

Charting Your Career
The Horoscope Reveals Your Life Purpose

Stephanie Jean Clement

Clients repeatedly ask astrologers for help with career decisions. *Charting Your Career* provides a unified, elegant, and comprehensive method for analyzing a birth chart and considering the impact of current conditions on career. You will find a fresh approach and new insights, based on the author's psychological and astrological counseling practices.

This book will help you to define your own creativity, see the best path to career success and identify how your skills and life experience fit into the vocational picture. It will help you to understand why your present job is not satisfying, and what you can do to change that. It can help you see where you may have missed opportunities in the past and how to make the most of new ones as they arise. It even shows what kind of building is best for you to work in! Finally, you can see your larger spiritual mission in light of your work abilities.

1-56718-144-9, 208 pp., 7½ x 9⅛   **$12.95**

Composie Charts
The Astrology of Relationships

John Townley

How does the world see you as a couple? Will your battles bring your closer together or waste your time? What is the best way to keep the romance alive? The composite chart describes that special dynamic that makes a couple more than the sum of its two personalities. It is a new, mathematically produced horoscope made up of mutual midpoints between the natal charts of two individuals.

Composite Charts is the definitive work on relationship dynamics by the "father of the composite chart," who has spent more than twenty years developing the technique he introduced in 1973. It incorporates a systematic theory of how and why composite charts work, comprehensive sections on composite planets in signs, houses, and aspects, as well as on the interplay of the natal charts with the composite chart they form, revealing who runs what within the relationship—or whether the relationship itself runs its progenitors.

1-56718-716-1, 528 pp., 7½ x 9⅛   **$24.95**

Alive and Well with Pluto
Transits of Power and Renewal

Bil Tierney

Pluto's path of deeper self-understanding is not an easy one, and its rewards do not come quickly. But when you learn to consciously confront this dynamic part of your psyche that otherwise remains dark and intimidating, you'll find a gold mine of psychological strengths that can help you face the world and maybe even transform it.

Learn how to better master the most complex areas of your life. Pluto's energy is intent on having us overcome our fears and self-doubts in favor of finding bolder and more passionate ways to express who we really are deep down inside. *Alive & Well with Pluto* offers new ways of looking at any personal life-dilemma you may fear is impossible to resolve—and does so in ways that will both entertain and enlighten you.

1-56718-714-5, 264 pp., 6 x 9 $12.95

Signs of Mental Illness
An Astrological and Psychiatric Breakthrough

Mitchell E. Gibson, M.D.

Signs of Mental Illness presents a provocative breakthrough in the sciences of astrology and psychiatry, demonstrating the use of new astrological techniques for diagnosing mental illness. Psychiatrist and astrologer Mitchell E. Gibson, M.D., uses scientific statistical research models to prove the correlation between astrological indices in a client's chart and the propensity for mental health or illness.

All the patients depicted in Dr. Gibson's study were diagnosed according to DSM-IV criteria, the gold standard of psychiatric diagnostic criteria. The diagnostic groups represented represent the most common causes of mental and emotional suffering: major depression, anxiety, addictive disorder, schizophrenia, and attention deficit disorder.

No previous astrological experience is needed to use Dr. Gibson's techniques. You will learn the declinations and multiple planet aspects that form the basis of this pioneering work.

- Learn to detect depression, anxiety, addictive disorder, schizophrenia, and attention deficit disorder in the a client's chart
- See the astrological markers for mental illness in the charts of Princess Diana, Saddam Hussein, Charles Dickens, Mike Wallace, and others
- Includes a basic course in astrology for newcomers to the science

1-56718-302-6, 216 pp., 6 x 9   **$14.95**